D1391091

4/12 £5-99

URBAN JUNGLE

THE SIMPLE WAY TO TAME YOUR TOWN GARDEN

Monty Don

HEADLINE

Also by Monty Don

The Prickotty Bush
The Weekend Gardener
The Sensuous Garden
Gardening Mad

Copyright © 1998 Monty Don

The right of Monty Don to be identified as the Author of this Work has been asserted by him in accordance with the Copyright, Designs and Patents Act 1988.

First published in 1998
by HEADLINE BOOK PUBLISHING

10 9 8 7 6 5 4 3 2 1

All rights reserved. No part of this publication may be reproduced, stored in a retrieval system, or transmitted, in any form or by any means without the prior written permission of the publisher, nor be otherwise circulated in any form of binding or cover other than that in which it is published and without a similar condition being imposed on the subsequent purchaser.

British Library Cataloguing in Publication Data
Urban jungle: the simple way to tame your town garden
1. Gardening
I. Title
635.9

ISBN 0 7472 2190 1

Designed by the Senate

Typeset by Letterpart

Colour reproduction by Radstock Repro

Printed and bound by Rotolito Lombarda, Italy

HEADLINE BOOK PUBLISHING
A division of Hodder Headline PLC
338 Euston Road
London NW1 3BH

To Sarah

Author's Acknowledgements

Lindsay Symons at Headline has been angelic in being encouraging throughout and tolerating my chronic inability to meet any deadline. Carole McGlynn edited my text with great sensitivity towards both writer and reader. Thanks to Jon Roseman and especially to Allasonne Lewis for creating time and constant support. As ever, thanks to Sarah Pearson for supporting and organising both myself and my wife Sarah. It is good to thank my Sarah for identifiable work for a change – she researched the pictures – but, as with everything that I ever do, the biggest debt of thanks is for always encouraging me with everything that has integrity and for being wholly intolerant of any bullshit.

Picture credits

The publisher would like to thank the following photographers and agencies for their kind permission to reproduce the photographs in this book:

David Askham (Garden Picture Library) page 156; Jon Boucher (GPL) page 13; Clive Boursnell (GPL) page 155; Lynne Brotchie (GPL) page 73; Linda Burgess (GPL) pages 25, 120, 163; Rex Butcher (GPL) page 15; Brian Carter (GPL) page 135; Densey Clyne (GPL) pages 65, 71; Karin Craddock (GPL) page 30; Henk Dijkman (GPL) page 49; Vaughan Fleming (GPL) page 26; Nigel Francis (GPL) page 47; John Glover (GPL) pages 22, 37, 43, 107, 110, 111, 115, 125, 157, 161; Sunniva Harte (GPL) pages 101, 187; Marijke Heuff (GPL) pages 45, 93, 147; Neil Holmes (GPL) page 139; Jacqui Hurst (GPL) pages 39, 56, 110, 113, 145, 175, 179; Andrea Jones (GPL) pages 117, 121; Phil Jude (GPL) page 173; Lamontagne (GPL) page 98; Jane Legate (GPL) page 29; A I Lord (GPL) page 119; S & O Mathews pages 17, 35, 51, 58, 59, 63, 67, 69, 72, 75, 78, 83, 86, 87, 89, 95, 97, 100, 116, 124, 164, 167, 171, 177, 189; Mayer/Le Scanff (GPL) pages 84, 152; Zara McCalmont (GPL) pages 10, 40; John Miller (GPL) page 61; Clive Nichols (GPL) pages 109, 183; Anthony Paul (GPL) page 23; Jerry Pavia (GPL) page 92; Howard Rice (GPL) pages 27, 36, 81, 103, 104, 109, 118, 123, 129, 138, 151; J S Sira (GPL) pages 55, 57, 105, 109, 127, 154, 160, 169, 185; Tim Spence (GPL) page 19; Ron Sutherland (GPL) pages 6, 16, 18, 19, 20, 24, 28, 33, 44; Nigel Temple (GPL) pages 144, 159; Michel Viard (GPL) page 141; Juliette Wade (GPL) pages 91, 181; Mel Watson (GPL) pages 126, 143, 149; Simon Wheeler page 133; Cynthia Woodyard (GPL) page 18; Steven Wooster (GPL) pages 46, 77, 158.

C    n t

e n t s

Introduction

IT SEEMS TO ME THAT THERE IS A LACK OF INTELLIGENT ADVICE BEING GIVEN TO SOPHISTICATED PEOPLE WHO HAVE GARDENS BUT ARE NOT IN ANY CONVENTIONAL SENSE OF THE WORD 'GARDENERS'. While you might not have the first idea of how to turn your garden into a beautiful place that is a daily source of creative pleasure, you have probably travelled widely, have a good job, the way your house looks matters to you and you exercise taste and discrimination over your choice of music, car, clothes and food. In other words you are not a complete idiot – just a gardening idiot. The point of this book is that all the main skills needed to garden are those you already have and use daily. I can give you a few hints and show you what *I* like, but in the end it is up to you.

There is a lot of rubbish talked about gardening, and misleading rubbish at that. For a start, it is really easy. Ignore the idea that you need to learn a whole series of facts and techniques, including hundreds of Latin names, before you can begin. You just stick things in the ground and they grow. The skills necessary to embellish on that are hardly horticultural. You do not need to pass an exam but simply to use the instinctive skills that you already exercise in other areas of your life. Gardening well is more to do with sensitivity to and awareness of your surroundings than to do with encyclopedic knowledge. If you are tuned in to the seasons and the properties of your own bit of land, with its vagaries of soil, climate and aspect, then you can hardly fail to grow most things more or less successfully. There are no hard and fast rules, just advice and tips gleaned from experience that people like me can dish out to save you time. By far the most useful lessons will come from your personal experience.

Another point that is never properly explored is *why* people garden. Too much emphasis is put on the tidiness factor, of treating gardening like housework in order to save face with the neighbours. This is like reducing interior design to washing-up or carpet cleaning. There are lots of complicated reasons for gardening – not least the British social need to aspire to a rural seat – but the best reasons are a combination of making a private landscape and the atavistic desire to grow things. If gardening is not creative and fun then it is a boring waste of time, and there are better ways of wasting time.

You must work out what you like and try and make it happen in the garden. It will take time and involve some mistakes; I do not believe in quick fixes. 'Instant' gardens are as enduring and banal as instant food. There is no hurry – one of the main reasons for gardening is to tune in to the rhythm of the seasons, the weather and the rate at which plants grow, flower and reproduce. It is a mistake to see the garden in terms of a picture with a finite end. Creating a garden is an ongoing process and it changes all the time. Plants grow amazingly fast and in my own experience time is always short. Do the basics properly and you will find a rate of transformation that may be more than you can cope with. And I do not believe in labour-saving for the sake of it – what is wrong with a little hard work?

I now garden in the country and love it. But for ten years I gardened in Hackney, in London, and I enjoyed that too. In a funny way I miss the restrictions and limitations of a town garden and the contrast between the street in the front of the house and the lushness of our garden out the back. So I know what it is like to live city life to the full *and* to make a town garden that you love.

It can and should be done.

(LEFT) Many town houses have three or more floors and the aerial view is an important part of the way that the garden is perceived.

Where to begin?

SO YOU HAVE DECIDED TO HAVE A GO AT THE GARDEN. YOU *WILL* MAKE SOMETHING OF IT. BUT WHERE DO YOU BEGIN? The first thing is to work out exactly what you want from your garden. It is no use digging it all for flower beds if its prime use will be as a playground for your children. Likewise, it is daft to put half of it to grass if you want a sensuous retreat. Think of your ideal garden and use that as both starting point and goal. There are design and style principles that can be taken from much larger, even palatial, gardens, and successfully applied on a small scale.

There is likely to be a series of requirements common to all urban gardens. Privacy is important to everyone and ideally there should be part of your garden that is as private as your bedroom. You cannot relax fully and feel unselfconscious about the creative side of gardening if someone is looking over your shoulder all the time. Town gardens must be retreats, so peace and calm matter a lot. But more important than anything else is that the garden is personal and idiosyncratic. It should feel at least as personal as your living room and in my opinion there is scope for far greater individualism out of doors than within.

I MADE THE FOLLOWING LIST OF REQUIREMENTS ON THE BASIS THAT EVERY TOWN GARDEN:

- Must be very organised spatially

- Must be structurally tight and formal, with no areas left undecided

- Must have at least one area of luxuriant planting

- Must have a ruthlessly selected choice of plants

- Must have soil that is as healthy as possible

- Must have space for sitting, eating and a good number of pots

- Must be geared around eating at a table

- Must have an irrigation system (at least an outdoor tap), however small

- Must always look good and inviting from inside the house

- Must contain at least one surprise

- Must be able to hibernate from November to Easter

- Must be robust

DIVIDE AND RULE

A SMALL GARDEN MUST BE DIVIDED INTO SMALLER SPACES IN ORDER TO MAKE IT SEEM LARGER. This is the key – break it down until it will go no further, then treat each division as a separate area that works harmoniously within the whole. If one area – and we could be talking of a section the size of a table top – does not work or is spoilt by a bit of bad planting, then the whole garden is not ruined. This approach has its drawbacks: it involves much more work than a more unified plan and it can get fiddly. But the beauty of a small garden is that it responds wonderfully to time put into it and half an hour spent on one tiny area can transform it. All effort is productive. And if it goes wrong you simply change it.

Many town gardens are long and thin, a shape which is ideally suited for dividing across its width by fences, hedges, walls or different levels. The resulting divisions do not have to be even as long as they are wide as they can create a new axis of interest, taking the eye across the width, with a seat on either side. Thus a garden measuring 20m x 10m (60 x 30ft) could have three quite distinct sections and each section be divided into two to allow for the inevitable variation in light that this would create, with one side in sun and the other in shade. Avoid curves unless you feel absolutely sure that they are the right thing in the right place, as they can often look dreadful. My advice is to stick to straight lines for the layout and structure and let plants do the softening. Do not make the mistake of having small borders in a small garden. It simply results in the garden feeling pinched. Generous borders will make the garden seem much bigger. Other than space to sit and eat, every spare inch should be given to growing plants.

Of course it is not easy to get the design right first time. There is a danger of crossing the line from intensity to clutter. But half the fun of gardening is the constant striving to get it right, to achieve that magical, but invariably fleeting, moment when plants and garden become Eden, your back garden giving a momentary glimpse into heaven.

One way of reducing clutter is to eliminate all the ordinary 'filler' plants that occupy space. A small garden is the perfect excuse to jettison them all and to restrict yourself to plants that you like, to varieties that perform best and are in some way special to you. New gardeners tend to assume that a dahlia is a dahlia and that tulips vary only in colour, but the undoubted secret of planting success is to identify the right plant for the space, from the huge range of nuances and differences between species and forms, both natural and specially bred.

This does not mean reducing the number of plants. Given the amount of care that can be lavished per square inch, it is possible to cram a surprising number of plants into a small space. Every book will tell you to leave a decent area around each plant to allow for growth and adequate nutrients, but ignore that. Prepare the ground well (see page 12) and then pack them in cheek by jowl. As individual plants get too big, you take them out or move them. This is part of the constant process of adjustment and tinkering in which gardeners find great pleasure.

An outsized object or plant can look perfectly at home in a tiny space as long as you are ruthlessly selective about it. If it does not look absolutely right, then get rid of it. There is literally no room for compromise. Of every individual plant, every paving stone, each pot, you must ask yourself whether it makes the best use of that particular space, or whether it is the right thing in the wrong place.

Even the tiniest garden is never static and will take any amount of rearranging and fine-tuning, in a way that is just not possible in a larger garden.

Assessing your plot

BEFORE YOU CAN BEGIN, YOU MUST BECOME INTIMATELY ACQUAINTED WITH YOUR GARDEN. This means more than peering at it out of the window. Take stock. Really look at it and try to identify the plants already growing there. See which ones are healthy and which look scrawny. The plot might be full of weeds. If they are big and vigorous, that can be good news as it implies that the soil is rich.

Notice where the sun is when you get up, in the middle of the day and in the evening. This will be the single most important influence on your garden. Evening sun in particular is a precious commodity. Start to think of organising your eating and seating area around where the evening sun falls, rather than around the house.

Take pictures of the garden to help you observe it objectively and to capture certain moods and light. If you have a polaroid camera it is perfect for this. Measure the garden by pacing it out.

Draw a scale plan onto graph paper and plot in all the existing hard features like manhole covers, walls and paths. Overlay it with tracing paper and draw on to this all existing large plants like trees, shrubs and climbers. This is a very good way to get to know your garden and you will be surprised at how different the information on the plan seems to your direct three-dimensional experience. Sketch out ideas and overlay them onto the basic scale drawing on another sheet of tracing paper. Be ambitious about this. It is easier than you might think to move paths, cut down small trees, plant hedges or build walls.

When the plan feels right, transfer it to the garden with string and sticks, stretching a length of string wherever there is a line. I love this stage and find it very exciting. Live with the result for a few weeks, adjusting things as you see fit. Then once you are happy with it, begin to lay down the 'skeleton', meaning all the hard bits and the permanent planting like trees, and hedges and grass.

Think of your garden as an extension of the house, as much a part of your living space as the kitchen or a bedroom.

Preparing the ground

IT IS IMPORTANT TO KNOW YOUR SOIL: EVERY SOIL HAS ITS OWN CHARACTER AND CONDITION AND THESE WILL LARGELY PREDETERMINE THE PLANTS THAT DO BEST IN YOUR GARDEN. LOOK AT NEIGHBOURING GARDENS. If you see pines, rhododendrons, birch trees, camellias and heathers, the soil is likely to be acidic. If you see beech hedges, lilac, clematis and yew hedges, then it is likely to be alkaline. Acidity and alkalinity in soil is measured by its pH factor and you can buy simple soil testing kits which will determine the pH for you. If it measures less than 6, your soil is acid and more than 7, it is alkaline. Most gardens fall somewhere between the two, but you need to know as you cannot make an acidic soil alkaline and vice versa.

Test for drainage by digging a hole 1m (3ft) in diameter and 30cm (1ft) deep. Pour in a bucket of water and see how long it takes to drain. If the water is gone within 10 minutes, then your soil is exceptionally fast draining and will need plenty of organic material, in the form of garden compost or rotted-down manure, to beef it up. If it takes more than an hour, it is either heavy clay or waterlogged. Heavy clay needs the addition of lots of organic material as well as sand or grit to help loosen it up. Waterlogged soil is rare and needs draining, for which you will need professional advice.

I cannot stress too strongly how important it is to lavish time, trouble, money and care on your soil. Soil is literally the basis of everything in the garden and you cannot have a successful garden without good soil. Town gardens may be full of builder's rubbish and all this will have to be removed before you start. Modern gardens are often turfed over, beneath which you may find heavily compacted soil, which is disastrous. Don't be lazy. Dig your flower beds deeply and add as much garden compost, rotted-down manure or whatever organic matter you can get hold of as you can. Mulch it thickly every spring by spreading a layer of organic matter – such as rotted manure or compost – at least 5cm (2in) deep over bare ground. The soil is the living body of the garden and the plants its clothes. If the body is healthy the garden will look good – whatever you plant in it.

It might seem drastic to dig a garden up but unless the soil is well prepared plants will never grow well.

The skeleton

The hard bits

SOMEWHERE DOWN THE LINE, GARDENING HAS BEEN HIJACKED BY PLANTS. A hierarchy became established by which the more that you knew about plants the 'better' the gardener you were judged to be and in the process a lot of very worthy but boring gardens, filled with 'good' plants, were created and revered. In fact you don't need to know a great deal about plants in order to make a beautiful garden, and it is quite possible to have a lovely garden filled with very ordinary plants.

The truth is that everything in the garden is important to the gardener. A pair of wonderfully planted borders with an ugly path running between them makes the whole garden ugly. For the first five years of a garden's life, the walls, fences, paths and patios are going to be the most visible aspects of it, so the first consideration is that they should look good. This inverts the normal consideration of function before form but in a small garden you need to take as much care with the choice of non-plant material as the plants. In a large garden you can hide mistakes and concentrate on the good parts while you make changes or plants mature. This is a luxury you do not have in a small garden, which looks only as good as the least successful bit.

Having said this, everything has to do its job well. Trellis needs to remain standing in all but a hurricane (I recall the Great Storm of 1987 ripping out all the trellis on my garden walls, although, curiously, it did not damage any of the climbers attached to it), paths must not subside and patios have to be level. Making sure that these features are well made and in working order is all part of gardening and, if done in the spirit of making your own fine and private place, they cease to be a chore to be got out of the way before the 'real' gardening can begin, and become essential elements of a creative whole.

Finally, remember that the garden *is* a whole. All the hard materials must relate to each other in exactly the same way as the different fabrics in a room. Avoid busy mixes of materials. If you are making a brick path, try and tie in the bricks you choose to the bricks of your house. If you have a path leading to a patio, they are both likely to look better if made from the same material. Keep things simple.

Two very different ways of using hard materials. (LEFT) Decking and an overhead grid to support climbing plants is modern and spacious, and (RIGHT) the mixture of pebbles and paving around an urn is more classical and intimate.

Fences and walls

WE INHERIT OUR PARENTS, OUR LOOKS AND, FOR THE MOST PART, OUR FENCES. They might be rickety, ugly, too low and deeply depressing, but we tend to feel that they are as immutable as the walls of the house. Wrong. There is no rule to stop you getting rid of anything in a garden that offends you. I suspect that you would not keep the last owner's wallpaper, or their bathroom fittings, in your house just because they were there, and neither should you tolerate any aspect of a garden that can be changed.

Many gardens have a mishmash of fencing panels, low walls, wire fencing and hedges marking their boundaries. This can have its own charm but usually looks a mess. Yet you cannot take everything down and start again because of the sensitivity of boundary demarcations and ownership of the structures. In my experience it is better to sacrifice a foot of territory and put up the wall or fence that you want to live with than to tolerate an ugly compromise.

Given the choice, a wall always makes a better permanent barrier than a fence. It looks more handsome, lasts longer and the sense of solidity it gives to a garden is a powerful influence. If you have the means, I would say that a wall was money well spent. But for many this is hardly an option. Walls are expensive, fences much cheaper. Do not underestimate the cost of a fence, however: a fence 2m (6ft) high is going to cost between £15 and £20 per metre in length.

The first job of a garden fence or wall would seem to be to mark your boundaries and establish your domain, although millions of American households manage quite happily without any sign of division at all. It seems to me that we have a human need for enclosed, private spaces – especially in an urban environment. The same fence that encloses your private space also keeps things out – neighbours, prying eyes, wind, dogs or footballs. To do this effectively it has to be tall enough and firm enough. You can erect a fence or wall up to 2m (6ft) tall without planning permission and I would suggest that this is the minimum height for privacy. If you are lucky enough to have taller boundary walls than that, then value them highly.

THE BEST KIND OF FENCE

To KEEP OUT THE WIND – which is the single most limiting element influencing the speed and manner of a plant's growth – you need a barrier that baffles the air rather than simply deflects it. Put simply, wind climbs over a solid wall and comes down the other side of it harder than ever, creating a wind-free zone at ground level only twice the height of the wall. If you have garden walls half as tall as your garden is wide, then that is fine and dandy. Otherwise a hedge or fence does a better job. The best windbreak is a woven hurdle, made from hazel or willow. These are light, easy to put up and, I think, look terrific. They are also more expensive than some other fences and have a life expectancy of only 5–10 years, so they are best used to protect a growing hedge; by the time the fence has rotted and broken, the hedge will be fully grown. For this reason hurdles are very effective for an instant barrier within the garden. A trellis fence – especially if the trellis is made of thicker wood than some of the flimsier types designed for attaching to a wall – also works well in the same role as internal divider and windbreak.

Larchlap panels are the most common fencing and are cheap – which is why they are ubiquitous – and nasty. But they can be made to look a lot better by nailing trellis to each panel, which will also help any climbing plant to smother them. Close-board fencing panels look much better and are stronger. They are made from vertical boards nailed to supporting cross-rails, so that there is a clear front and back to the two sides. Whichever fencing you choose, it will only be as strong as the supporting posts. Hurdles are normally fixed to round posts hammered into the soil but all other fencing has to be fixed to posts set in concrete to hold them firm and straight.

If you wish to increase your privacy but do not want to offend neighbours, try putting up a trellis extension to the existing fence or wall. The initial effect is to preserve visual contact while increasing the sense of enclosure but climbing plants can quickly cover the trellis to make a more solid barrier.

The combination of gravel and uneven stone is always pleasing. I like the gravel island in the middle of the stone surface.

Paths

PATHS ARE MUCH UNDERVALUED ELEMENTS OF A GARDEN. Every garden has paths and they influence the way it looks and behaves just like any other more obviously horticultural component and a great deal more than some. Paths define spaces as much as hedges or walls, and in the same way that roads define towns and countryside for the traveller. They invite you down them, a fact which anyone designing a garden should use to help in unravelling the space to the visitor's eye.

I also like the way that function and form are so inextricably bound in a path. If you want the quickest route to or from the garden shed or compost heap, the chances are you will be moving purposefully and carrying something and the path needs to be a generous, uncluttered line. If you are drifting round a herb garden, choosing a bit of this and a sprig of that, the path is better narrow and broken by barriers and turns, so the surface can afford to be busier and more decorative.

LAYING A PATH

IF A PATH IS TO SURVIVE YEARS OF FROST AND RAIN, LET ALONE NORMAL GARDEN WEAR AND TEAR, YOU HAVE TO MAKE IT PROPERLY.

- First dig out the path-to-be to a depth of at least 23cm (9in).
- Then edge the sides with boards, attached to pegs driven into the ground.
- A path through grass should be set below the level of the turf to make mowing easier, but, if flanked by borders, the edging boards should be at least 5cm (2in) above the surface of the path to stop soil spilling onto it.
- Then put at least 15cm (6in) of hardcore or rubble on the bottom. This must be roughly levelled and then tamped down. On top of the hardcore spread 3–5cm (1–2in) of sand and rake it level before laying the final surface of bricks or stone.
- This is the basis for any hard-surfaced path, of brick, tile or stone. When you have finished a section, mix up a weak, dry sand and cement mortar (6:1) and brush it between the joints before sprinkling with water.

A gravel path needs exactly the same preparation up to the tamped-down hardcore. This should then be covered with a porous layer – of crushed scalpings (the waste product of quarries) or some stone mixed with a clay base so that it will set hard. The secret of a good gravel path is to spread the gravel very thinly so that it is just a stone thick over the sub-layers; this stops it spreading around and feeling like a sand dune to walk through.

Crushed bark is an ideal surface if you have toddlers who are always falling over. The path can be marked out and edged with boards but not dug out and the bark simply poured in 5cm (2in) deep. It will be very easy to convert this into something more permanent after a year or two.

If you use bricks, they must be laid in a pattern or bond that suits the site and purpose of the path. If the bricks are laid as stretchers across the path it has a regular rhythm that suits a long, wide stretch. If they are laid lengthways, you will find yourself compelled to move along it faster. Basketweave is busier and best for shorter stretches, and herringbone is busier still. Brick is also very good as a constant among other mixed materials. Either have a ribbon of brick down each side of a path and infill with whatever you have to hand, or create a repeated pattern which the brick ties together.

Patios

WHEN PLANNING A PATIO it is helpful to think of the word's original meaning in Spanish, which is an inner courtyard open to the sky. This is a complete description of many good town gardens and the patio should be the focus around which a small garden is created.

A patio is primarily an organised space for eating outside – a practice that one should indulge in at every opportunity – and while it is usual to unthinkingly attach a paved area to the house so that it forms a link between indoors and out, it is vital that your patio should be sunny at the time of day you will use it most. The sun will not obligingly direct itself where you want it, so you must go to it. It is pointless to have a carefully designed sitting area bathed in morning sun while you are out at work and in deep shade by the time you want to eat your evening meal outside. One of the advantages of a small garden is that carrying a tray of food to the end of the garden can be a positive pleasure if the path is flanked by good planting. So always site your patio where the sun is, even if that means putting it at the furthest point from the house.

The surface must be firm, level (although with a very slight slope to take surface water away) and dry. This is likely to mean stone, brick or wooden decking, laid over a base of levelled hardcore and sand. Be generous with the space – you can always cover an 'extra' area with pots. But allow room for planting, at the edges especially, to create a sense of privacy. The actual planting style will range with your taste, but I think that this is not the place for obsessive minimalism or austerity. A sense of luxuriance is more conducive to relaxed eating and drinking. Scent is vital to the enjoyment of food and the musky opulence of the tobacco plant (*Nicotiana sylvestris*), summer jasmine (*Jasminum officinalis*) or scented-leaf geraniums is very suitable.

If the patio is away from the house, raise the height of the fence or walls with trellis and cover them with screening plants such as *Vitis coignetiae*, *Clematis montana* or *Wisteria sinensis*. If you have good walls (an advantage of having a patio attached to the house), then clothe them with climbers that will flower at the time of year you will use the patio most, which is likely to be from May through to October (see pages 54–69).

PATIO SURFACES

YORK STONE
Looks good anywhere but is expensive and heavy to handle.

BRICKS
Huge range of colour and texture. Easy to handle and lay but old bricks are liable to crumble after frost.

IMITATION STONE SLABS
Uniform size, easy to handle and cheap, as well as being remarkably authentic, but they never look quite as good as the real thing.

GRAVEL
Cheap and easy to lay, although not ideal for a patio: too harsh and irritating a surface and not stable enough for furniture.

WOODEN DECKING
Ideal for covering drains, or existing concrete. Involves no excavating, is relatively cheap and can look very good. Slippery when wet.

MIXED SURFACE
Can work well if used with discretion. Remember that the most visible area is around the perimeter, not in the centre.

TIP

A tip for laying York stone:
Measure each piece of stone and number it with chalk. Then draw each stone to scale on a sheet of paper, cut out the pieces and work out the best arrangement for the flags in the space available. This will save you much time and an awful lot of hard labour.

(LEFT) Stone flags of various sizes mixed with brick make a rhythmic surface with multiple textures contrasted (RIGHT) with the minimal but powerful juxtaposition of stone curves and wooden lines.

LAYING A PATIO

1 Dig out the area to a depth of at least 30cm (1ft).

2 Hammer in pegs in a 1m (3ft) grid, using a straight edge and spirit level to get their tops level. Make sure that the surface is at least 15cm (6in) below the damp-proof course of the house. Remove any soil where needed to give at least 23cm (9in) clearance to the top of the pegs.

3 Fill in with a layer of hardcore at least 15cm (6in) deep. Level off and tamp down firmly.

4 Cover the hardcore with a 5cm (2in) layer of sand.

5 Lay your final surface on this, using more builder's sand to maintain correct levels. Start on the patio's longest side and work across, butting stones and bricks tightly together and making sure each piece is level before laying the next.

6 Brush a 6:1 mixture of dry sand and cement into the joints and spray lightly with water.

Steps and levels

VERY FEW GARDENS ARE ABSOLUTELY LEVEL and many town gardens are on a very steep slope indeed. This can make life very difficult, ruling out wheelbarrows and turning a trip to the end of the garden into an expedition requiring ropes and crampons. But it also makes for a very interesting garden. In Where to Begin? (page 8), I speak about the need for dividing a long narrow garden to create different spaces and make it seem bigger. Steps are both a form of division in themselves and work very naturally used at the gap in a more solid divider like a hedge, fence or wall.

Even a very gentle slope can provide the opportunity to make a couple of steps through the technique known as cut and fill. You dig into the slope and use the excavation and the spoil to create the steps. If you have a bank you will have to cut into it to make the steps, digging them out and compacting them firmly. The risers can be made of wood, stone or brick but must be securely fixed, with the bottom one on a firm base. Infill the gaps created between risers with hardcore, topped with a layer of sand. The riser for each step sits upon the stone or brick of the lower step.

Be generous with the width of steps – you want two people to be able to walk side by side, which requires about 1.5m (5ft) to be comfortable. It is important to get the depth of the tread right as well. Too shallow and you have to walk up on tiptoes; too deep and you lunge at it. There is a formula which declares that the depth of the tread plus double the height of the riser should total about 65cm (26in). If you have steps on the main path in your garden it might be a good idea to divide the steps with a narrow brick slope running down the middle, just wide enough for the wheel of a barrow. It looks good too.

If you are gardening on a steep slope, this gives an opportunity to terrace the garden, with each terrace defined by retaining walls. This is quite a big project – but no more difficult than digging a large pond. There are only two important things to remember and the rest is common sense. The first is to keep topsoil separate. Mixing subsoil and topsoil does not improve subsoil – it just ruins topsoil. The second is to provide plenty of drainage both through the retaining walls and down the terraces themselves. A slope is often very exposed to wind, so provide plenty of shelter, especially if it faces east or north.

(LEFT) Strong planting around steps distracts from their steepness, whereas (RIGHT) the change in levels is accentuated by flanking box plants and pots.

The echoing green

EVERY GARDEN IN THE NORTHERN HEMISPHERE IS BUILT OUT OF GREEN MATERIALS. This can be hard to believe on a grey winter's day, when the streets and buildings seem to crush the light and life out of every growing thing, but green is the colour upon which the garden rests. Once you understand this, then you must set about constructing the garden from green materials. This goes against the grain for the first-time gardener who wants sensual colour and exuberance, but without their backdrop of green these are mere random splashes. The more urban the garden setting, the more important green becomes in creating an oasis of calm and rest. Green is the symbol of life and vitality and we all physically and psychologically need it in our lives – so never underestimate its power within the palette of your garden.

I could be very happy in a garden where *all* the plants were green. I would have green hedges – both evergreen like yew and deciduous like hornbeam – infilled with luminous grass and a variety of trees and green 'architectural' plants. It would be certainly limited but never boring, because although green remains reassuringly constant throughout the year, it does change with the seasons. Think of the shining, translucent green of May, the plump rich green of July on the same plants and, if evergreen, their matt refusal to fade in the middle of winter.

The green in a garden comes from three sources: evergreens such as holly, yew, ivy or pine trees, which keep their leaves all the year round; deciduous plants whose leaves fall each autumn and grow anew each spring and, lastly and definitely least, green flowers. Some of these are stunning, such as the apple-green petals of the Corsican hellebore (*Helleborus argutifolius*), or the lime-green of *Zinnia* 'Envy' and the soft green flowers of bells of Ireland (*Molucella laevis*). Green has the widest range of perceptible shades of any colour, running from almost black to almost yellow. With experience and a little planning you can begin to use this range with subtlety to build a shifting tapestry of rich effects in the garden without ever stepping out of the green embrace.

Define the shape of your garden in green. Use low green hedges such as box, lavender, rosemary or sage. Mark the corners, entrances and focal points with green trees and bushes. Use taller green hedges to create enclosures and volumes or compartments within the garden. It does not matter how small the garden is – even a window box can be structured with greens.

(LEFT) The honeybush *Melianthus major* has perhaps the best leaves in the garden but (BELOW) cardoon (*Cynara cardunculus*) is also fantastic – and much hardier.

Lawns

I MUST PREFACE ALL THAT FOLLOWS ON THE NEXT FEW PAGES BY SAYING THAT I THINK THAT LAWNS ARE A BAD IDEA IN ALMOST ALL SMALL GARDENS. However, I like lawns for all the reasons that everyone else likes them: they feel good underfoot, are great to lie out on, look tremendous when freshly cut and add the perfect green link between areas of colour. But . . . consider the downside. For over half the year they are muddy and uninviting. They need cutting but hardly warrant the expense or storage of a mower. A perfect lawn is quite tricky to make and maintain and it will not support tables or chairs. My advice is to convert an existing lawn to a paved area, which will look as attractive, be used the year round, is no more trouble than a lawn to lay (although more expensive) and needs practically no maintenance. The only time a town lawn is applicable is if you have small children or it is there primarily as a visual effect. But if you still want your lawn, this is what you do . . .

MAKING A LAWN

PREPARATION IS THE KEY. IT IS A SIMPLE EQUATION: THE BETTER PREPARED THE SOIL IS BENEATH THE GRASS, THE BETTER THE GRASS WILL LOOK. FOR THE SIZE OF LAWN MOST SMALL GARDENS HAVE, THERE IS NO REASON NOT TO PREPARE IT THOROUGHLY.

- Dig it over just as you would a border, removing all stones and weeds, including every scrap of root.

- If the soil is at all heavy, it is worth adding as much sharp sand or grit as you can. Spread it as a layer over the soil and lightly fork it in. This will help drainage, the lack of which is the biggest problems in most lawns.

- Level it with a rake but do not attempt to get too fine a surface yet. Leave it for at least two weeks, which gives any weeds left a chance to grow so that they can be removed.

- Rake the soil again, this time getting it as level and fine as possible. A level lawn (not necessarily flat, but even) always looks good. The grass will not hide any dips and hollows, and it is much easier to get it properly level at this stage.

- Tread over it with your heels, compressing the surface, then rake it again in both directions. It is now ready for sowing or turf.

Rolls of turf (RIGHT) make an instant visual surface but the ground needs as much preparation as more naturalistic grass (LEFT).

Turf or seed?

THERE ARE ADVANTAGES AND DISADVANTAGES TO BOTH TURFING AND SOWING A LAWN. On balance I would plump for turf if you can get a good supply (use a large, reputable garden centre or find a turf merchant through the Yellow Pages) and your lawn is in an open, sunny site. If you have a larger area, the lawn is in shade or you are not certain about the quality of the turf, go for grass seed, buying a mix that meets your requirements in terms of wear and suitability for shade or sun.

- Seed is much cheaper.
- Turf gives an instant effect.

- Seed is easy to sow.
- Turf must be laid very carefully.

- Seed can be stored and sown when it suits you.
- Turf cannot be stored and must be laid within a day or two of delivery.

- A sown lawn cannot be used for about 10 weeks.
- A turf lawn can be used after about 4 weeks.

- Seed needs watering in dry weather.
- Turf needs a daily soak.

- Seed is eaten by birds and scratched up by cats.
- Turf isn't vulnerable to either.

- You can control the type of seed to suit the precise needs of your garden.
- Buying turf can be a lottery.

Here grass is used at the end of the garden as an enticement whilst a more practical paved area is used nearer the house for eating and sitting.

SOWING SEED

1 Scatter seed evenly over the prepared, level ground, and rake it in.
2 Protect it from birds using cotton thread or, for a small lawn, plastic netting.
3 Water it with a sprinkler except on rainy days.
4 Watch it grow and do not worry if it seems to be growing patchily or thinly. It will thicken up very fast over the course of a few months.

LAYING TURF

Water the soil the night before laying the turf.

1 Start at one corner and work across the site in a line, using a plank to stand on to avoid spoiling the surface of the soil, and butt the edges of the turves (squares of turf) tight together.
2 Start the next row, staggering the joins of the turves like a course of bricks, keeping them tightly together, and tamping them down flat. Use another plank to avoid standing on the turves you have already laid.
3 Keep all short pieces of turf in the middle, trimming them to fit with a sharp knife, so that there are no small bits of turf at the edges.
4 Water the laid turf thoroughly and keep it watered every day until it starts to grow. Do not step on it at all for at least a month.

Let the grass from both seed and turf grow longer than you would normally have it for the first season, not cutting it until it reaches about 5cm (2in), when it can be cut back to 2.5cm (1in) and maintained at that length for the remainder of the season. The best time to sow seed or lay turf is September, which gives it time to grow before winter and makes the fact of a no-go area less inconvenient. By the following spring it should be established and ready for use. Otherwise sow or lay turf in spring.

MAINTAINING YOUR LAWN

● One of the most common problems with lawns is lack of drainage, followed by lack of sun. Grass likes very free drainage and sunshine to grow well and while no lawn likes badly drained soil, it is possible to buy grass seed for shady areas. Drainage can be improved by spiking the lawn with a fork and spreading sharp sand over the lawn, brushing it into the holes, in spring or autumn. This, I warn you, is a lot of work.

● Another common cause of problems in lawns comes from cutting them too short. Grass is much healthier when kept a little longer than the average lawn owner is used to. It is also better to trim off a little each time rather than make one drastic cut.

● When you make the first few cuts of the year, collect the grass clippings. As the weather gets warmer and drier, clippings can be left on the ground and will actually help the grass in dry periods. Always collect them after the last cut of the autumn.

● Spread grass cuttings thickly around the base of trees and hedges as a mulch to stop weeds growing and retain moisture. Always mix cuttings with a dry material like shredded paper, straw or leaves before adding them to the compost heap, otherwise they turn into a green, evil-smelling sludge.

● Rake the lawn in spring and autumn with a wire rake to remove the thatch or dead grass and to aerate the soil.

Foliage plants

A FOLIAGE PLANT IS ONE GROWN PRIMARILY FOR THE BEAUTY OR USEFULNESS OF ITS LEAVES. 'Usefulness' sounds horribly utilitarian but many plants are very important as buffers between other, more dramatic ones and come into their own when grown as groups, where the effect is greater than the sum of the parts. Hedges are the most obvious example but this also applies to individual plants such as cotoneaster, lavender, santolina, moss, ground-covering periwinkles or the wide range of grasses that can be grown as border plants.

As for beauty, one is spoilt for choice. Plants like cardoons (*Cynara cardunculus*) or the tender but lovely *Melianthus major* have large, dramatic leaves which would justify the space needed for the plant even if it did not flower. Hostas do flower wonderfully but are grown by most people for their leaves alone. Almost all ferns have lovely fronds despite some, like the male fern *Dryopteris filix-mas*, being able to thrive in the driest shade.

Within the essential green hue of most foliage lies a huge spread of colour. My favourites tend to be glaucous (a grey/blue shade of green) which can appear to be silvery, blue or pale green depending on the light. Foliage in this colour range makes a very good foil for flowers too. Some plants have leaves that are almost yellow until you see them next to a true yellow flower. These plants are very good for introducing light into a shady area, where they thrive away from direct sunlight which has a tendency to scorch them. Any plant with 'aurea' as part of its Latin name is likely to have a yellowish cast to it. More common are yellow and green variegated plants. Variegation is tricky to use – too much two-tone becomes fuzzy and distracting – yet that same softness of focus can be harnessed to lighten an otherwise dark or tonally dull area.

Of course foliage does not only come in shades of green. Purple leaves have a powerful role to play in the garden but because of their strength they should always be used sparingly. The best purple-leaved plant for my money is the purple hazel (*Corylus maxima* 'Purpurea'). This should be cut right down to the ground every two or three years and in response it will throw up vigorous straight branches whose very dark purple leaves make an excellent backdrop in a large border. I hate the purple-leaved 'Pissard's plum' (*Prunus cerasifera* 'Pissardii'), which is a dead colour in leaf and a tangle of branches in winter.

GLAUCOUS-LEAVED PLANTS

Artemisia abrotanum
Cynara scolymus (artichoke)
Cynara cardunculus (cardoon)
Echium candicans
Eryngium alpinum (sea holly)
Hosta sieboldiana
Lavandula angustifolia (lavender)
Melianthus major
Santolina chamaecyparissus
Sedum spectabile
Stachys byzantina (lamb's ears)

YELLOW-LEAVED PLANTS

Carex elata 'Aurea' (Bowles' golden sedge)
Hosta 'Sum and Substance'
Choisya ternata 'Sundance'
Filipendula ulmaria 'Aurea' (meadowsweet)
Lamium maculatum 'Cannon's Gold' (dead-nettle)
Lonicera nitida 'Baggesen's Gold'
Melissa officinalis 'Allgold' (lemon balm)
Origanum minutiflorum 'Norton Gold' (yellow marjoram)
Ribes sanguineum 'Brocklebankii' (flowering currant)

VARIEGATED PLANTS

Cornus alba 'Elegantissima' (dogwood)
Euonymus 'Emerald 'n' Gold'
Euphorbia characias wulfenii 'Emmer Green'
Ilex aquifolium 'Golden Milkboy' (holly)
Hosta 'Ground Master'
Hosta fluctuans 'Variegated'
Mentha suaveolens 'Variegata' (pineapple mint)
Miscanthus sinensis 'Variegatus'
Pulmonaria rubra 'David Ward' (lungwort)
Symphytum x *uplandicum* 'Variegatum' (variegated comfrey)

PURPLE-LEAVED PLANTS

Corylus maxima 'Purpurea' (purple hazel)
Heuchera micrantha diversifolia 'Palace Purple'
Sambucus nigra 'Guincho Purple' (purple elder)
Dahlia 'Bishop of Llandaff'
Cotinus coggygria 'Royal Purple' (smoke bush)
Ocimum basilicum 'Purple Ruffles' (purple basil)

When hedging is edging

IT IS A VERY COMMON — BUT DISASTROUS — MISTAKE TO THINK THAT THE RIGID CONFINES OF URBAN GARDENS ARE MADE LESS RESTRICTIVE BY INTRODUCING CURVES. The opposite is true. The smaller the garden, the greater is the need for some tightly defined structure, and it is my firm conviction that a successful small town garden rests upon the framework of formal planting – and this means, among other things, the use of small hedges to create spaces and patterns.

From the first water gardens of Persia to the first quarter of the eighteenth century, it was understood that gardens needed a formal framework to establish balance and order. Then along came William Kent, Capability Brown, Humphrey Repton *et al* and swept this away at the large country houses to which every Englishman desperately aspired. Sad. There has been a partial revival of formal gardening, with recreations of 16th-century knots and sub-Versailles parterres, but there is no need laboriously to ape historical precedent to learn from it. The most straightforward lesson is that the same plant or small group of plants used in geometrical patterns establish a harmony and balance that invariably make the garden look better.

The trick is to use low hedges to create empty spaces that you can then fill as chaotically or as starkly as you fancy. In winter the geometry takes over and in my opinion looks wonderful, and in summer it does not matter if it is all but submerged beneath the weight of flowers. Indeed, the restrictions imposed by the hedges seem actually to increase the sense of abundance.

I like to think of these spaces as three-dimensional rather than in plan, so they are boxes to be filled rather than a chequerboard. One way to turn this from an intellectual idea into hard reality is to make the low hedges not quite as low as a lot of pictures suggest. The best example of perfect proportions that I know of is the famous White Garden at Sissinghurst in Kent. Although it is part of a very grand estate, it is extremely useful as a guide for the small garden. The area is subdivided into a series of small spaces by box hedges which I guess to be 1m (3ft) high, whereas most similar hedging is restricted to 60cm (2ft) or even 45cm (18in). These may sound insignificant figures but the overall difference to the look of a garden is huge.

Box is by far the best plant to use for low hedges. It positively relishes being clipped and in a couple of years you can achieve and maintain a really crisp edge to it. It will also grow from bare wood, so if damaged it can be cut hard back and will reliably regrow. It grows slowly so needs clipping only once or twice a year, it is tough, very long lasting and will grow in deep shade. There are two types to consider, *Buxus sempervirens* and *Buxus sempervirens* 'Suffruticosa'. The latter is much slower growing than *B. sempervirens* and much more expensive. To achieve the 'boxed' effect I have described you must use *B. sempervirens*. This can be allowed to grow taller at chosen intervals, such as the corners of each 'box', and then clipped to form a shape such as a cone, pyramid or ball.

If you want softer edges, or simply to create a contrast with the emerald-green of box (as was common in Elizabethan knots), use santolina, hyssop, rosemary, lavender or thyme, all of which will create small herbal hedges. I often use parsley as a temporary edging plant to line a path – making it easy to pick for a calendar year before it goes to seed and bolts.

THE MOST USEFUL FORMAL EDGING PLANTS

Buxus sempervirens (box)

Santolina chamaecyparissus

Hyssopus officinalis

Rosmarinus officinalis (rosemary)

Lavandula angustifolia (lavender)

Thymus x *citriodorus* (lemon–scented thyme)

Petroselinum crispum (parsley)

Immaculately cut low box hedges make the ideal framework to contain flower beds.

Grasses

FORGET LAWNS. There are much better ways of using grass to good effect in a small garden. There are hundreds of different grasses, from the fine bents found in lawn seed, such as *Agrostis tenuis*, to giants like the bamboo *Phyllostachys vivax* or huge stands of pampas grass (*Cortaderia selloana*).

Because they do not have flowers in the obvious visual sense (yes, I know they really do have flowers but you know what I mean), it is the shape, colour and, above all, the *texture* of grasses that is so powerful. I love *Helictotrichon*, for example, which we grow in terracotta pots. It keeps its colour all year round and can be clipped to make a very satisfactory ball of glaucous hedgehog spikes. *Carex flagellifera* feels exactly like a hank of silky hair when

you run your fingers through it, and both squirrel-tail grass (*Hordeum jubatum*) and *Molinia caerulea* are worth growing for their feel alone.

A clump of grass sounds pleasing too, whispering gently in the summer wind, with delicate grasses like *Stipa tenuifolia* and *Calamagrostis* catching the movement of even the faintest breeze and rustling with a drier sound in winter. For this reason alone, you should not cut grasses back in autumn but wait until their new growth is visible in spring.

Urban gardens are often too hard-edged, with brick walls, paths, patios and surrounding buildings overwhelming the plants. Grasses, with their arching yet contained growth, can do much to soften this harshness, particularly if planted along the edge of a path or against a wall. The fescues are some of the prettiest for this role and are easy to grow in rather poor, well-drained soil. They like sunny sites. *Festuca glauca* is the best known and very attractive, as is *F. mairii*.

Almost all grasses will cope with ordinary garden soil – which is to say soil that is dug deeply and has some organic material mixed into it – although there are grasses that will thrive in certain extreme conditions. Most grasses and all bamboos need plenty of water, especially for the first few years after planting, while they are getting established. Evergreen grasses need to have all the old foliage cut to the green at the beginning of spring, before the new shoots get too tall.

Grasses are easily replenished by division. The time to do this is when the plant is growing most vigorously, which is spring or early summer. Dig up the plant, and, with a sharp spade, chop it into two or three pieces, replanting each of them in their new positions in well prepared soil. A word of warning – some grasses such as the sedge (*Carex riparia*) or *Phalaris arundinacea* are very invasive and are best kept to containers in small gardens.

(LEFT) Ornamental grasses look very good in a mixed border or (RIGHT) as individual plants in a container, like this *Festuca glauca*.

FAVOURITE GRASSES
Agrostis nebulosa (cloud bent)
Calamagrostis x *acutiflora* (feather-reed grass)
Carex flagellifera (brown-leaved sedge)
Cortaderia selloana (pampas grass)
Festuca glauca (blue fescue)
Festuca mairii (Maire's fescue)
Helictotrichon sempervirens (blue oat grass)
Hordeum jubatum (squirrel-tail grass)
Molinia caerulea (purple moor grass)
Phyllostachys vivax 'Aureocaulis' (fishpole bamboo)
Stipa tenuifolia

Architectural plants

ARCHITECTURAL PLANTS ARE DEAD TRENDY, but I have to admit that it took me ages to find out what these plants actually were before I realised that I had them all along. So much for fashion. Nevertheless it is a handy term to describe plants that make a visual effect through their form rather than their flowers or leaves. Another and perhaps more helpful way of looking at the 'architecture' of a garden is to identify the plants that are important to you, the key plants that you want in your garden. The resulting architecture that they are shaping is intellectual as much as physical, but that is no bad way to view a garden – it should exist as vividly in your mind as it does outside your back door.

Architectural plants are therefore a personal group and can come from the whole gamut of plant life, from annuals to trees. But the accent must be on the whole plant, rather than any feature or detail of it. Hybrid Tea roses, for example, have some wonderful (as well as downright horrible) flowers but tend to be spiky, ugly plants for eight months of the year. If they did not flower, no one would grow them, so clearly they could never be used as an architectural plant. This is not to dismiss roses, however

– many shrub roses with their much more profuse growth and arching stems, make excellent architectural plants.

With the rare exception of a large tree, no plant stands completely alone in a garden. Its impact and form is always set within the context of its surroundings – and you, the garden-maker, define that context. Do not dot these key plants about carelessly, even in the most informal of gardens. Place them at the end of a vista, at the corner, in the centre of or at equal spacing along a border. Think of these plants rather like the main pieces of furniture in a room. If you have a very loose, sprawling garden, then the key or marker plants can have the same looseness of form – a shrub, cardoon or small tree might well fit the bill. If however you have a more formal layout, then a clipped evergreen or a plant that has a compact, symmetrical habit would work better. Evergreens have the advantage of working their effect throughout the year, coming forward more forcibly in winter. But deciduous plants, perennials and annuals can be equally important as long as their performance coincides with what is happening around them. It goes back to setting everything into the context that you want.

(RIGHT) *Acanthus spinosus* grows in sun or shade, tolerates drought and produces wonderful spires of flower as well as its distinctive foliage. A superb plant.

EVERGREEN ARCHITECTURAL PLANTS
Buxus sempervirens (box)
Ilex aquifolium (holly)
Laurus nobilis (bay)
Mahonia aquifolium
Taxus baccata 'Fastigiata' (Irish yew)

STRUCTURAL ANNUALS, BIENNIALS AND PERENNIALS
Acanthus mollis, A. spinosus
Angelica gigas
Carex elata 'Aurea' (Bowles' golden sedge)
Cynara cardunculus (cardoon)
Foeniculum vulgare (fennel)
Hosta sieboldiana
Kniphofia 'Prince Igor' (red-hot poker)
Levisticum officinale (lovage)
Melianthus major
Onopordum acanthium (Scotch thistle)
Phormium tenax
Rheum x *hybridum* (culinary rhubarb)
Verbascum olympicum (mullein)
Yucca filamentosa

SMALL TREES AND SHRUBS WITH EXCEPTIONAL SHAPE
Acer (maple)
Catalpa bignonioides (Indian bean tree)
Chaenomeles japonica (flowering quince)
Laburnum x *watereri* 'Vossii'
Magnolia stellata
Malus 'Golden Hornet' (crab apple)
Pyrus salicifolia 'Pendula' (silver-leaved pear)
Robinia pseudoacacia 'Frisia'

Topiary

TOPIARY CAN SEEM TO BE RATHER A
SPECIALIST ASPECT OF GARDENING, but it really
only refers to the simple shaping of plants. You can, of course,
take that to extremes and there are amazing examples of topiary
in which horses, riders and a pack of hounds pursue a fox along
the top of a hedge, all in yew. But any simple, clipped shape is
topiary.

Topiary is an extremely effective way of punctuating and
emphasising entrances, paths, the corners of borders or patios,
steps or vistas. A pair of identical balls, cones or pyramids placed
on either side of a path, whether in pots or planted in the
ground, immediately gives it a sense of theatre. A series of shapes,
perhaps standard balls ('standard' in gardening always refers to a
tree with the trunk left clear of branches to a certain height) in
a line along a border, will give it substance in summer and form
in winter. Study any good, seemingly carefree garden and you
will notice topiary shapes all over the place.

You can buy topiarised shapes ready formed, but they are very
expensive and it is simple and good fun to make them yourself.
The trick is to direct the plant into a configuration that suits its
natural tendency. Almost all plants respond to clipping by
growing denser, but box more so than any other plant, so it
makes very good solid shapes such as cones and pyramids. Yew
behaves in the same way but is also good to train, as its very
flexible branches are easy to tie and bend and they grow rigid
over a few years. Holly is ideal for making 'poodles' or 'wedding
cakes', which refers to the layered pom-poms and tiered
cylinders into which holly is usually cut. Experience has shown
some plants to be more suitable for topiary than others. These
are, in order of user-friendliness:

- *Buxus sempervirens* (box)
- *Taxus baccata* (yew)
- *Ilex aquifolium* (holly)
- *Crataegus monogyna* (hawthorn)
- *Prunus lusitanica* (Portuguese laurel)
- *Lonicera nitida*
- *Ligustrum ovalifolium* (privet)
- *Laurus nobilis* (bay)

Flat planes are harder to cut true than curves, so start out on
circles or cones rather than squares and pyramids. Cut timidly at
first, establishing one plane or curve, then matching the rest to it.
I find that I have to take two or even three 'passes' at each bush
to get it dead right. A common mistake with topiary (or any type
of pruning) is to think that the tree will steadily increase in size
while still maintaining its clipped shape. Plants do not work like
that. They only grow outwards from new growth. The advantage
of this is that you can always rectify mistakes. The disadvantage is
that you can accidentally snip off an important piece of the
developing shape.

Another common mistake is to leave a 'weak' area of a shape
uncut so that it can grow and fill out. This goes against all the
basic rules of pruning which is that the harder you cut, the
stronger the subsequent regrowth. Clip any loose, open pieces
back hard, reducing the scale of the whole piece to match if it is
young. It will look like a plucked chicken for a month or two,
but will soon come back as you want it. If a mature piece of
topiary gets damaged, cut back the broken branches and leave
them to regrow to fill the hole.

The best time to clip topiary shapes is late summer. This
enables them to recover from the trauma (it upsets them) before
winter and look crisp until their new growth starts the following
spring. If your plant is very vigorous and you do not want it to
grow any bigger, it might need another trim the following May.

Topiary is very low-maintenance gardening. This standard box *(Buxus sempervirens)*
clipped to a lollipop shape will only need an annual trim - as will the lavender below it.

Ground cover

GROUND COVER IS A CATCH-ALL TERM TO DESCRIBE PLANTS WHOSE PRIMARY PURPOSE IS TO BLANKET THE SOIL IN GROWTH – usually foliage. The main reason for doing this is to control weeds, because bare soil will inevitably fill with weeds unless it is constantly weeded. (It is worth remembering that if your garden has lush, vigorous weeds, there is a silver lining in that this is a very good indication of the fertility of the soil.) By covering the ground you are depriving emerging weed seedlings of light, which will kill most of them. The second reason is to provide a controlled, harmonious link between plants, other than bare soil. It is important to differentiate between the two kinds of ground-cover plants: the first spread over the top of the ground like a kind of living mulch, such as periwinkle (*Vinca*), and the second kind are invasive plants like the ornamental sedge (*Carex riparia* 'Variegata'), grass or bluebells which, once established, are almost impossible to remove.

The downside of ground-cover planting is also twofold. Aesthetically it can look very boring and municipal and is often completely unsuitable for the average small garden. In practice, ground cover can exceed its original brief and take over, becoming a weed itself. There is a delicate balance because a plant that is sufficiently vigorous and spreading to be useful as ground cover is likely to become too vigorous, once established.

Ground-cover plants do not need to be small. The only prerequisite is that they grow sufficiently thickly to dominate a position and blanket out the light. So rhododendrons or bamboos make good ground cover, and the most common and effective ground cover that appears whenever there is a bare patch of ground in the British countryside are brambles. Perhaps the best ground cover of all is grass and there was a trend in larger gardens to plant shrubs in grass for exactly this reason. I think this always looks really ugly and, speaking from forced experience, it makes the grass a nuisance to cut.

The regular cutting of ground cover can work very well indeed, however, if you use a woody, prostrate shrub and trim it with hedgecutters or shears once a year. Ivy, cotoneaster, prostrate juniper (*Juniperus* x *media* 'Pfitzeriana') and rugosa roses all do the job well, especially on a slope. The inexorable non-woody spreaders like the dead-nettle (*Lamium maculatum*) are best kept under control with shears or else they go berserk and take over the whole garden.

Although the aim is to suppress weeds, it is very important to dig the site and weed it very thoroughly before you plant your ground cover. Resist the temptation to plant too close together as this will weaken the plants' growth and not help the eventual cover. It is better to allow individual plants sufficient space to develop strongly and to this end you must keep even the most vigorous spreaders free from weeds for the first year, while they establish.

(FAR RIGHT) There is no mystery to ground cover - any single laterally growing plant or an assortment of plants that block out weeds will do the job.

GROUND COVER FOR DRY, SUNNY PLACES
WOODY
Artemisia abrotanum
Ceanothus 'Cascade'
Cistus x *cyprius*
Cytisus 'Moonlight' (broom)
Juniperus procumbens
Lavandula angustifolia
Rosmarinus officinalis 'Prostratus'
Salvia officinalis (sage)
Santolina chamaecyparissus (cotton lavender)
NON-WOODY
Acanthus mollis
Achillea millefolium 'Cerise Queen' (yarrow)
Aubretia x *cultorum* 'Purple Cascade'
Tanacetum parthenium (feverfew)
Geranium renardii
Nepeta 'Six Hills Giant' (catmint)
Sedum spectabile
Stachys byzantina (lamb's ears)
Teucrium fruticans (germander)

GROUND COVER FOR DRY SHADE
WOODY
Buxus sempervirens (box)
Fatsia japonica
Hedera hibernica (ivy)
Hypericum calycinum
Prunus lusitanica (Portuguese laurel)
Berberis wilsoniae
NON-WOODY
Blechnum chilense (hard fern)
Euphorbia amygdaloides robbiae
Lamium maculatum (dead-nettle)
Waldsteinia ternata
Vinca major, V. minor (periwinkle)

GROUND COVER FOR MOIST SHADE
Anemone blanda
Hosta 'Shade Fanfare'
Hypericum calycinum
Tiarella cordifolia (foamflower)
Pulmonaria 'Sissinghurst White', *P.* 'Blue Ensign'

GROUND COVER FOR LIGHT SHADE
WOODY
Fargesia nitida (bamboo)
Cotoneaster atropurpureus
Elaeagnus pungens
Escallonia 'Donard Seedling'
Hypericum 'Hidcote'
Rhododendron 'Hatsugiri'
Vinca minor (periwinkle)
NON-WOODY
Ajuga reptans (bugle)
Alchemilla mollis (lady's mantle)
Bergenia 'Bressingham White'
Geranium 'Ann Folkard' (cranesbill)
Hemerocallis (day lily)
Saxifraga x *urbium* (London pride)
Symphytum (comfrey)

Trees and hedges

THERE IS A TENDENCY TO REGARD TREES AND HEDGES AS FIXTURES THAT ARE AS UNCHANGEABLE AS THE WALLS OF THE HOUSE ITSELF. This is not so. An ugly or inappropriate hedge can be cut back and dug out in a day and a tree in half that time. By the same token it is never too late to plant. Do not be intimidated by the time it takes a hedge to grow from a straggle of individual plants to a crisp-edged barrier. Half the secret is to plant trees and hedges properly so that they grow fast, and the other half is to enjoy them as they grow. Flowers can be made to repeat themselves year after year, but the pleasure of trees and hedges is that they allow a garden to evolve and change each season over a human lifetime.

One of the common delusions about trees is that they have a finite form that takes a long time to reach and are therefore not worth bothering with in a small garden. But this is as crazy as thinking that a child is only an adult in the process of forming. To get the most out of a tree you have to realise that it is as much a complete tree from the moment you plant it as a child is a complete person. It will grow surprisingly fast and, if you plant it properly and keep it watered, you will be astonished at how quickly the sapling of 1.5m (5ft) you planted will become a 6m (20ft) tree.

It is worth remembering that a hedge is just a group of trees planted in a row and trimmed regularly. However, in a small garden the two perform very different roles. A solo tree will add height and substance and give shade as well as an important quality of maturity or permanence to a garden. A hedge, on the other hand, has an orchestrated effect, accumulating in large gardens to create grandeur. While a small town garden is no place to have delusions of grandeur, there is hardly a garden that cannot be improved by the addition of a hedge.

Here I must confess a bias. I love hedges. To me they symbolise everything that is good about a garden: a living, changing structure that is controlled and tamed to help create the fantasy that every garden should be. The most obvious practical uses of a hedge are as a boundary or screen to provide privacy. But they are also invaluable for dividing the garden into separate spaces. It has become a cliché to talk of garden 'rooms' but, like all clichés, it is founded in a useful concept, one that can be surprisingly effective even in a very small garden. For an outdoor domestic space to feel comfortable it should be related in scale to the human body, just like rooms in a house, and dividing a small space also has the effect of making it seem larger.

You can, of course, divide space with walls and fences and the effect will be instantaneous. But a hedge adds a whole range of textures – of leaf, of light filtering through, of bare branches in winter, of birds nesting in it, of the wind rustling through it – and creates a satisfyingly three-dimensional substance.

(LEFT) This entire Edinburgh garden revolves around one tree to brilliant effect.
(RIGHT) Even two trees in a line create a sense of ordered division and rhythmic spacing.

Choosing trees for small gardens

WHEN SELECTING A TREE FOR A GARDEN THERE ARE A NUMBER OF DIVERGING OPTIONS TO CONSIDER. Do you want it to grow naturally or will you shape it? Should it be flowering or not? Deciduous or evergreen? Single specimen or a group?

In a small garden a single specimen tree is going to have to work hard for its space and must therefore be chosen carefully. You want at least two of the following qualities: attractive leaves, flowers, scent, interesting bark, toughness and ease of cultivation, an intrinsically good shape, as well as the ability to respond well to shaping or pruning. A group of trees is almost always going to be pruned and trained to make an effect, be they a series of clipped yews, trained limes or hornbeams or a screen at the end of the garden. As I have covered topiary on page 40, I will concentrate here on specimen trees.

I love blossom. When that is combined with fruit, a tree becomes extra valuable and many fruit trees make very suitable specimen trees in a border. Pears flower slightly earlier than apples, making them more susceptible to damage by late frosts – a point worth considering if you live in a cold area. Apples and cherries both flower in early May and are tough. Medlars flower very prettily and their fruit makes good jelly. No fruit tree is ever grown on its own roots but is grafted onto the roots of another species, like crab apple, quince or hawthorn, to control its growth. The size of the tree is thus dictated by the rootstock onto which the variety is grafted. These rootstocks are codified by number. Make sure you buy an apple on M106 or M111, which are sometimes sold as half-standards or standards. This enables the trunk to grow sufficiently high (2m/6ft before the first branches)

for you to grow plants under it and to sit or eat in its shade.

Do not think that a small garden must have tiny trees. You can always prune a tree to reduce its size. And as for dwarf conifers – their attraction baffles me. But each to their own.

FLOWERING TREES FOR SPRING
Crataegus 'Paul's Scarlet' (hawthorn)
Magnolia kobus
Malus sylvestris (crab apple)
Prunus 'Kanzan'
Sorbus (many)

FLOWERING TREES FOR SUMMER
Aesculus hippocastanum (horse chestnut)
Catalpa bignonioides (Indian bean tree)
Laburnum
Magnolia grandiflora

FLOWERING TREES FOR AUTUMN
Acacia dealbata
Magnolia campbellii (*will not grow on lime*)
Prunus mume
Prunus x *subhirtella* 'Autumnalis'

GOOD AUTUMN FOLIAGE
All maples (*Acer*), including field
   maple (*A. campestre*)
Betula (birch)
Ginkgo biloba
Prunus sargentii
Quercus rubra (red oak)
Sorbus

(LEFT) These trees frame the path like an arched roof over a nave – with as grand an effect as any cathedral.
(RIGHT) Trees filling a window frame make a perfect combination of inviting space and absolute privacy.

Planting a tree

PLANTING A TREE OF ANY TYPE INVOLVES PREPARING THE PLANT FOR A VERY LONG JOURNEY. While with smaller plants you can often get away with just sticking them in a hole, planting properly really matters with a tree. Writing down the stages involved in planting makes it seem a palaver, but it is neither complicated nor difficult and will make a huge difference to the way that the tree grows, especially in the first five years.

- Dig a hole the depth of a spade and 1m (3ft) in diameter, putting the soil to one side. If this topsoil is not rich and crumbly, you will have to make it up with potting compost.
- Loosen the next layer of soil with a fork to the same depth again, breaking it up into crumbs so that the roots can easily grow through it. If you have rotted manure or compost, add a generous layer and mix it in well.
- Place the tree in this hole, spreading out the roots. Position a supporting stake so that it does not damage any root but is close enough to attach to the trunk of the tree. Remove the tree and bang in the stake.
- Replace the tree as it was, either loosely attaching it to the stake or with someone else holding it upright. Carefully sift the topsoil around the roots, concentrating on filling in all the spaces. When all the roots are covered, tread the soil down firmly with the full weight of your body. The ground will subside quite a lot when you do this.
- Add more topsoil until the level is 2.5cm (1in) below the ground and then water it in, using at least 10 litres (2 gallons) of water. This is both to provide the tree with liquid and also, equally importantly, to work the soil into any gaps around the roots.
- Let the water drain and mulch with a 5cm (2in) layer of compost around the full radius of the hole.

GROWING TREES IN A CONTAINER

ALMOST ANY TREE WILL GROW IN A CONTAINER IF IT HAS ENOUGH ROOM FOR ITS ROOTS TO DEVELOP AND IS WATERED AND FED SUFFICIENTLY. This is an especially good way of growing trees that need a different soil to that of your garden. In principle the pot cannot be too big, but in practice you should aim for a pot with a width equal to one-fifth of the tree's height. The implication is that you need to put it into progressively larger pots as it grows or keep it pruned to a certain height. Make sure the bottom of the pot has plenty of drainage crocks or pebbles, use a potting compost specifically for trees and shrubs and add a handful of bonemeal when planting. Leave at least 8cm (3in) of clearance between the top of the soil and the top of the pot to allow sufficient water to cover the roots. As with all trees, it is better to water generously once a week than little and often. Citrus are ideal trees for a pot, as are bay, Portuguese laurel, box and silver birch. Weeping trees can also look very good, such as weeping ash, weeping beech, weeping silver pear (*Pyrus salicifolia* 'Pendula') and weeping cherry (but *not* weeping willow, which grows too fast).

(RIGHT) *Robinia pseudoacacia* 'Frisia' makes the ideal town garden tree, with rich buttery leaves from spring till autumn.

Hedges

WHEN CHOOSING WHICH KIND OF HEDGE TO PLANT THE OPTIONS
DIVIDE INITIALLY INTO TWO TYPES, DECIDUOUS OR EVERGREEN.
Deciduous plants lose their leaves in autumn, leaving the branches bare all winter before growing
new leaves in spring, whereas evergreens retain their leaves all year round.

Do not be tempted into buying large hedging plants in the belief that this will make a mature
hedge faster. The opposite is nearly always true. The smaller the plants, the faster they adapt to
their new position and the stronger they grow. Only plant large specimens (i.e., over 1m/3ft tall)
for an instant effect and be prepared for very little growth for the first few years after planting.

Plants are priced largely by age, rather than size. A mature plant is expensive because of the time
spent looking after it. Therefore the slower a plant grows, the more costly it becomes, year on year.
Plants are also measured by height rather than width. So a tall, spindly plant will be more
expensive than a squat, bushy one, even though the latter is more valuable to you in the garden.
Always buy bushy young plants that will do their expensive growing in your garden rather than
in a nursery.

Be generous with your spacing when planting a hedge. The wider the plants are, the stronger
they will grow. Research has also shown that there is no advantage in planting a double row to
make a thicker hedge. A well-spaced single row will reach the same thickness in the same time
for half the cost.

(RIGHT) A yew hedge makes the best backdrop for any flowers,
be it a single rose bush in a pot, as here, or a large border.

Planting a hedge

CONTAINER-GROWN PLANTS CAN BE PLANTED AT ANY TIME OF YEAR. Bare-rooted deciduous plants should ideally be planted between October and April and preferably before Christmas, and bare-rooted evergreens in late spring (April or May) or early autumn (September or October). Whatever type of hedge you plant, and whenever you do it, the more thorough your preparation, the faster and stronger it will grow. The principle is exactly the same as for planting a tree (see page 48), save that you dig a trench rather than a round hole and a hedge will not need staking unless the plants are exceptionally tall and spindly. Ideally the trench should be 3 spade-widths (approx. 60cm/2ft) wide. This may seem like overkill when you realise how much soil has to be excavated, but it ensures a good root-run for the growing plants and will guarantee a healthy, fast-growing hedge. Mix in plenty of well-rotted manure or compost and add a handful of bonemeal for each plant. Water thoroughly after planting and mulch the whole trench with a generous layer of organic material.

Keep all new hedges as slim as possible, cutting the sides (i.e., front and back) narrower than their final profile. This will encourage them to thicken laterally as they continue growing up. But the most important factor in the aftercare of new hedges is to keep them watered. Your tactics to this end should be both adding water and reducing water loss. Even if it rains, remember that much rainwater will sit on foliage and evaporate before it can reach the roots. A thick mulch will stop evaporation but also reduce the effects of light rain which will not penetrate the mulch layer; perhaps more importantly it will stop weeds or grass growing around the roots, which would rob the hedge of available water, so keeping the hedge weed-free is vital in the first few years.

DECIDUOUS HEDGES

One of the most significant features of a deciduous hedge is the dramatic change that it will impose upon your garden. In midwinter it is almost impossible to imagine the naked branches wrapped in green leaves and then they seem so abundant and lush in June that the winter starkness that is bound to follow is equally unimaginable. This can be a strong plus point if you relish seasonal differences: for myself, I find fewer things more dynamic than the first flush of green leaves in the hedgerows in April. If on the other hand you want a constant framework or backdrop, an evergreen hedge is more appropriate.

Another consideration is hardiness. If you live in a very cold or exposed site, deciduous plants may grow better. They shed their leaves to avoid making demands for moisture on the roots during winter, so they effectively hibernate in bad weather, whereas an evergreen hedge has to support the demands of its green leaves whatever the weather or conditions.

EVERGREEN HEDGES

Town gardens need order, peace and controlled structure and evergreens are the prime providers of all these qualities throughout the year. A simple mix of evergreen hedges and grass can be enough to make a beautiful garden. Most evergreen plants are also tough and easy to grow. The only danger is winter dehydration and, other than keeping them watered, the best way to avoid this is to protect them from winter winds. A cold wind can kill plants that are otherwise healthy by drying them out, especially if the frozen ground stops any moisture from reaching the roots.

Yew (*Taxus baccata*), box (*Buxus sempervirens*) and holly (*Ilex aquifolium*) are the three native evergreens and make the toughest, best-looking evergreen hedges for any garden. All have a reputation for growing slowly – the worst modern horticultural crime – but my experience is that they will grow fast and bushily if treated well, yet need cutting only once a year.

Remember that while vigour might be desirable in a young hedge it becomes a definite drawback in a mature one, as the hedge will need cutting often. Privet (*Ligustrum*) needs trimming once every two months and Leyland cypress four times a year.

CUTTING HEDGES

Hedge cutting is only pruning by another name and the same two general principles of pruning apply, which are that summer pruning tends to restrict growth and summer is therefore the best time to cut any plant to shape, while winter pruning stimulates growth and is done to revitalise a plant.

With the exception of beech (*Fagus sylvatica*) and hornbeam (*Carpinus betulus*), all new deciduous hedges should be cut back to half their height immediately after planting. This will hurt you much more than it hurts them. But cutting hedge plants back will encourage them to respond with more vigorous, bushier growth so that the hedge will not mature with gaps at the bottom. Cutting back will also reduce the stress on the roots while they get established. Shorten the new growth by half once again, the following summer. Beech and hornbeam should not be pruned for the first two years, but then they can be cut back by one third to encourage the hedge to grow sideways and thicken up.

DECIDUOUS HEDGES

CARPINUS BETULUS (HORNBEAM)
- ☑ Vigorous and tough; lovely green summer foliage; holds its leaves all winter.
- ☒ None; best on heavy or poor soil.
  Plant at 45cm (18in) spacing.

CRATAEGUS MONOGYNA (HAWTHORN)
- ☑ Fast-growing, cheap; best for an informal or boundary hedge; wonderful blossom if left uncut.
- ☒ Thorny (which can be an advantage); scruffy in winter; needs cutting twice a year.
  Plant at 23cm (9in) spacing.

FAGUS SYLVATICA (BEECH)
- ☑ Good green colour in summer; holds its russet leaves all winter.
- ☒ Dislikes heavy soil; best on chalk.
  Plant at 30cm (1ft) spacing.

PRUNUS SPINOSA (BLACKTHORN)
- ☑ Good blossom in early spring.
- ☒ Vicious thorns.
  Plant at 30cm (1ft) spacing.

ROSA RUGOSA
- ☑ Lovely flowers in summer; fast-growing, very tough.
- ☒ Thorns and lax growth; best for an informal or boundary hedge.
  Plant at 60cm (2ft) spacing.

EVERGREEN HEDGES

BUXUS SEMPERVIRENS (BOX)
- ☑ Makes the best low (under 1.2m/4ft) hedge of all; very neat and compact; tough and long-lasting; very good for shaping.
- ☒ Expensive and slowish to reach more than 60cm (2ft).
  Plant at 30cm (1ft) spacing.

ILEX AQUIFOLIUM (HOLLY)
- ☑ Good barrier or boundary hedge; looks terrific.
- ☒ Prickly; not good for planting around as fallen leaves are painful for ages.
  Plant at 45cm (18in) spacing.

PRUNUS LUSITANICA (PORTUGUESE LAUREL)
- ☑ The toughest of all evergreens; will grow in total shade.
- ☒ Largish leaves mean hedge has to be largish to look neat.
  Plant at 60cm (2ft) spacing.

TAXUS BACCATA (YEW)
- ☑ A mature yew hedge makes the perfect green backdrop – any other evergreen hedge is second best.
- ☒ Expensive, slowish to mature; needs good drainage.
  Plant at 60–75cm (2–2ft 6in) spacing.

Growing up

Climbing plants

WALLS HAVE MANY PRACTICAL ADVANTAGES – THEY CAN SUPPORT AND SUSTAIN CLIMBERS, PROVIDE SHADE AND SHELTER FOR PLANTS (AND HUMANS) at their base, they hold heat like a storage heater and they don't need weeding or digging. Ask yourself what kind of display you want, in order to make the most of your walls.

Do you want a brilliant summer display – in which case a rose is likely to do the trick among other things – or do you want all-year cover with an evergreen? Will you have a number of smaller climbers, perhaps performing at different times of the year to give a succession of flowers, or do you want one superb lead-player throughout the season? Is the wall attached to the house or do you look at it from a window? Is it near where you eat outside or by a path? All these considerations should be borne in mind before planting.

The other important consideration is to know in which direction your walls face. A south-facing fence or wall will provide the ideal situation for a range of plants that would hate a north-facing one. Remember that the sun comes from the east first thing in the morning, from the south at midday and afternoon and sunset is in the west. A north-facing wall is in permanent shade. In a city you may well find other buildings blocking the sun, so that even your south-facing aspect is in shade for half the day.

PLANTING CLIMBERS

Whatever climber or wall shrub you choose, plant it with the same care, size of hole and amount of goodness as if it were a tree (see page 48). An extra 20 minutes spent when planting will transform the plant's performance and prolong its life by years. The flowers and leaves might be delicate but the height to which a climbing plant grows means it needs a lot of nourishment.

- Dig a hole 1m (3ft) in diameter and 30cm (1ft) deep.
- Loosen the lower layer of soil and add plenty of organic material in the form of well-rotted compost or manure.
- After planting the climber, water it in very well and mulch it with a thick layer of rotted garden compost.

CARE OF CLIMBERS

- Plant any climber as far from the wall as you have the space to do, up to 1m (3ft) away if possible. This will give the plant a chance to establish without competing with the wall for moisture and a chance for the rain to reach its roots.
- A fully grown climber is heavy, especially in full leaf, so however tiny the plant when you buy it, make sure that its support is securely fixed.

- When fixing trellis or wires to the wall as support, make sure that you fully anticipate the growth of the plant, providing support to the highest point that you want it to grow.
- Leave a gap of 5cm (2in) between the wall and trellis or wires to allow the climber to grow behind them and air to circulate.
- Be careful where you weed. Most feeding roots for climbers are near the surface, so do not be too energetic with a fork near the base of the plant.
- Climbers need feeding annually, so dress them with bonemeal or potash-rich fertiliser (such as any proprietary tomato fertiliser) every April, which will help in the production of flowers.

(LEFT) Evergreen *Clematis armandii* is deliciously fragrant and one of the best early spring climbers for a warm wall.
(RIGHT) The climbing rose 'Constance Spry' is here trained up a tripod but will grow equally well on a wall or trellis, and is also wonderfully scented.

South-facing walls

CONSIDER A VERTICAL SURFACE FACING SOUTH (and this is one of the minor confusions of garden-speak: a 'south wall' is actually on the north side of the plot but it *faces* south). It is going to get the full effect of the sun from mid-morning until early evening which is from 9am till 3pm in winter and 10am till about 6pm in summer. The north wind will not touch it and the east merely ruffle its feathers. These are the two cold ones so it is not just bright but hot. Not all plants like this and will scorch during a hot summer. It is exposed to winds from the south, which are invariably warm and drying, and fairly well protected from westerlies that bring rain. The base of a south wall, even after quite heavy rain, is a dry place. Not all plants are keen on that either, although a combination of enriching the soil, mulching the surface and the use of a drip irrigation system will solve the problem.

Roses on a south-facing wall will do well early in the year and at the end of summer but will not give of their best in midsummer – which is when most roses flower. Therefore choose early- or late-flowering roses for a south-facing wall. The brightness of the sun will bleach subtle colours, which often look better in thin morning light. Blues tend to look their best in evening light and I prefer oranges and rich reds in the low light of evening too. Fruit such as figs, peaches, grapes, apricots and pears will ripen much better against a south wall.

Whatever you do finally plant, give it plenty of goodness in the soil and as much space away from the wall as you have. The base of a south-facing wall is the driest place in the garden and only the heaviest rain will water it sufficiently for most climbing plants. Add lots of compost to the planting holes and mulch as thickly as possible. If you do not have organic material to hand for a mulch, stones make a good barrier against water-loss through evaporation. There is no shortage of plants that will grow on a south wall, so that wherever plants appear twice, this indicates that they have more than one distinct quality rather than spreading a limited choice thinly. Unless otherwise stated, the climbers listed overleaf are all summer-flowering.

(LEFT) *Ceanothus*, with its wonderful powder blue flowers, is best with the sunniest spot available.
(RIGHT) *Clematis tangutica* will flower almost till Christmas if given a protected, sunny site.

BEST PLANTS FOR SOUTH-FACING WALLS

EVERGREEN
Ceanothus impressus
Clematis armandii
Magnolia grandiflora
Trachelospermum jasminoides

SPRING-FLOWERING
Clematis armandii
Jasminum beesianum
Wisteria sinensis 'Caroline'

AUTUMN-FLOWERING
Ceanothus 'Autumnal Blue'
Eccremocarpus scaber
Jasminum officinale
Solanum crispum 'Glasnevin'

WINTER-FLOWERING
Chimonanthus praecox var. *luteus*
(wintersweet)

WHITE-FLOWERED
Jasminum officinale
Jasminum x *stephanense*
Rosa x *fortuneana*
Solanum jasminoides 'Album'
Trachelospermum jasminoides
Wisteria sinensis 'Alba'

YELLOW-FLOWERED
Chimonanthus praecox var. *luteus* (wintersweet)
Clematis tangutica
Humulus lupulus 'Aureus' (golden hop)
Rosa 'Gloire de Dijon'
Rosa banksiae 'Lutea'
Thunbergia alata (black-eyed Susan)

PINK-FLOWERED
Clematis armandii 'Apple Blossom'
Jasminum x *stephanense*
Schisandra chinensis
Wisteria floribunda 'Rosea'

BLUE-FLOWERED
Ceanothus
Rosmarinus officinalis (rosemary)

PURPLE/MAUVE-FLOWERED
Passiflora caerulea (passion flower)
Wisteria floribunda 'Violacea Plena'
Wisteria sinensis 'Caroline'

RED/ORANGE-FLOWERED
Campsis x *tagliabuana* (trumpet vine)
Eccremocarpus scaber
Jasminum beesianum
Lonicera x *brownii* 'Fuchsoides'

(RIGHT) Trellis is an ideal support for a clematis as its tendrils can wrap around the framework. If the trellis tops a low wall, as here, remember to plant the clematis well away from the wall and lean it back to the trellis via a cane.

FRUITING
Peach 'Peregrine'
Apricot 'Moorpark'
Grape
Nectarine
Fig 'Brown Turkey'
Cydonia oblonga (quince)

ANNUAL
Eccremocarpus scaber
Ipomoea (morning glory)
Passiflora caerulea (passion
flower)
Thunbergia alata

FAST-GROWING
Any evergreen ceanothus
Fallopia baldshuanica (Russian
vine – *very* vigorous)
Passiflora caerulea (passion
flower)
Wisteria sinensis (once it gets
going)

GOOD SCENT
Jasminum officinale
Jasminum x *stephanense*
Rosa banksiae 'Lutea'
Rosa x *fortuneana*
Solanum jasminoides 'Album'
Wisteria sinensis 'Alba'

East-facing walls

THE BEST-KNOWN RULE ABOUT AN EAST-FACING WALL IS THAT IT IS NOT A GOOD PLACE FOR DELICATE, EARLY-FLOWERING CLIMBERS. The reason for this is that in cold weather it will have been cooling since midday, making it prone to any frost that is about. The frost itself will not damage hardy flowers but a cold spring night is often followed by a bright morning and the first light that shines directly onto the climber will be intensified by the layer of ice around the flowers and will scorch them. By the time the much hotter sun reaches a west-facing wall – which might have been just as frosty – the frost will have melted and no damage will be done. Not all plants are afflicted (for example, flowering quinces shrug off any combination of ice and sun) but camellias in particular are prone to this type of damage and should not be planted on an east wall except in the mildest areas, even though they will flower very well on it.

East-facing walls receive – in theory – the same amount of sunlight as a west-facing one but it does not feel that way because the type of sunlight is so different. The delicacy of morning light is best suited to soft colours and all the pastels, yellows and whites as well as the cooler blues, look at their best planted where they catch the morning sun. But an east wind is anything but delicate, chilling humans and plants alike with a dry, insistent blast and, combined with the dangers of scorching, it makes an east wall one of the hardest places for which to find plants that will flourish. Furthermore, an east wall changes its character throughout the year. In the middle of winter it is in shade almost all day, whereas in summer it is potentially bright from 5am until after lunch. Its post-prandial shade provides a soothing coolness and suits plants like clematis or roses perfectly well. Actually both types of plant are, in my experience, pretty tough and cope well with a huge variety of positions.

Much more important to the gardener is how plants will look in the context of their garden rather than how suitable the position for the plant is. The more delicate the colouring of any flower the less likely it will be to fade if grown up an east wall. For clematis, particularly those that flower after June, the lack of moisture against an east wall is a bigger problem than the lack of sun. The same is true for most honeysuckles (*Lonicera*) that are happy to have their roots in shade while the flowers reach upwards towards whatever light is going. An east wall is fine for all but *Lonicera etrusca* and *L. sempervirens*, which are best protected by a south wall. When grown in shade, a honeysuckle is less likely to get attacked by aphids, which can afflict it sorely.

EVERGREENS
Choisya ternata (Mexican orange)
Garrya elliptica (tassel plant)
Hedera (ivy)
Hydrangea petiolaris (climbing hydrangea)

SPRING-FLOWERING
Chaenomeles (flowering quince)
Clematis macropetala
Clematis montana
Forsythia suspensa

SUMMER-FLOWERING
Lathyrus latifolius (perennial sweet pea)
Lonicera tellmanniana (honeysuckle)

AUTUMN-FLOWERING
Lonicera periclymenum
'Graham Thomas' (common honeysuckle)

WINTER-FLOWERING
Jasminum nudiflorum (winter jasmine)
Lonicera fragrantissima (winter-flowering honeysuckle)

Honeysuckle is ideal for an east-facing wall or fence.

WHITE-FLOWERED
Rosa 'Climbing Iceberg'
Rosa 'Mme Legras de St Germain'

YELLOW-FLOWERED
Forsythia suspensa

PINK-FLOWERED
Roses: 'New Dawn'; 'Gypsy Boy';
'Louise Odier'; 'Zéphirine Drouhin'

BLUE-FLOWERED
Clematis macropetala 'Lagoon'

PURPLE/MAUVE-FLOWERED
Clematis x *jackmanii*
Clematis 'Gypsy Queen'

RED/ORANGE-FLOWERED
Rosa 'Guinée'
Tropaeolum speciosum (flameflower)

FRUITING
Chaenomeles (flowering quince)
Cotoneaster (fishtail cotoneaster)
Prunus (Morello cherry)
Pyracantha rogersiana (firethorn)

ANNUAL
Tropaeolum speciosum (flameflower)
Runner bean

FAST-GROWING
Clematis montana
Humulus lupulus '*Aureus*' (golden hop)
Runner bean

GOOD SCENT
Clematis montana
Lonicera periclymenum
   'Graham Thomas'
   (common honeysuckle)
Rosa 'Mme Legras de St Germain'

North-facing walls

A NORTH-FACING WALL GETS ONLY A FLARE OF WEAK SUN AT DUSK IN THE MIDDLE OF SUMMER AND NONE ALL WINTER. Not only is it dark but its brand of shade is cold and dry. But there are enough plants that relish these unlikely conditions to make it a backdrop for a number of interesting plants. It will never be somewhere that one chooses to sit and will always have rather an austere feel to it, but there are a number of flowering climbers that do well in the dark. They all tend to have white or very pale flowers for the obvious reason that this makes them more visible for would-be pollinators.

The ubiquitous and lovely *Clematis montana* is not often deliberately planted on a north wall but it will grow and flower there very well, giving a mass of scented flowers in May. The roses 'Madame Grégoire Staechelin' and 'Madame Alfred Carrière' are the two always quoted for dark walls although in my experience the best of all is the ruby-red 'Souvenir du Dr Jamain' which likes the cool shade. I have a pair growing in pots on either side of our north-facing back door, where they flower profusely. Two white Alba roses, 'Madame Legras de St Germain' and 'Madame Plantier' are deliciously scented, tough and guaranteed to flower in shade although for only about six weeks in June and July. The practically evergreen rambler, 'Albéric Barbier' is more ivory than white and is especially good if you have the space for it to ramble over.

Honeysuckles are woodland plants, evolved to grow in the shade of a tree and clamber up it in search of light. *Lonicera* x *italica,* which has creamy, beautifully scented flowers in summer, *L.* x *brownii,* with its scarlet trumpets in late summer, and *L. caprifolium* in early summer all feel at home on a north fence or wall. The winter honeysuckle (*L. fragrantissima*) is not really a climber but it can be pruned tight against a wall and a dry, north-facing one would be ideal. It has the best scent of all flowers.

There are a few plants, all suitable for a north wall, that need no support as they form rootlets where they make contact points with a surface. The most important are ivy, *Hydrangea petiolaris*, *Euonymus fortunei* and Virginia creeper (*Parthenocissus quinquefolia*). Of these the climbing hydrangea is the most handsome, with white flowers in mid- to late summer. It can be slow to get established but have patience and it will make good ground (or wall cover) after two or three years. The winter-flowering jasmine (*Jasminum nudiflorum*) will produce its buttery flowers on bare green stems in the deepest, driest shade. Like quite a few plants, this is more a case of tolerance than preference, but needs must when the deep shade drives. The same is true of the flowering quinces (*Chaenomeles japonica*) and camellias, although camellias will not grow on limy soil.

(ABOVE RIGHT) 'Souvenir du Dr Jamain' is one of the very few roses that performs much better in shade than sun, so is happy in a north aspect as long as it does not get too dry.

WINTER INTEREST
- *Euonymus fortunei*
- *Hedera* (ivy)
- *Jasminum nudiflorum*
- *Lonicera fragrantissima*

SPRING-FLOWERING
- *Clematis macropetala*
- *Clematis montana*
- *Clematis* 'Moonlight'

SUMMER-FLOWERING
- *Hydrangea petiolaris*
- *L.* x *brownii*
- *Lonicera* x *italica*
- *L. sempervirens*
- *L.* x *tellmanniana*
- *Rosa* 'Madame Alfred Carrière'
- *Rosa* 'Madame Plantier'
- *Rosa* 'Souvenir du Dr Jamain'
- *Rosa* 'Zéphirine Drouhin'
- *Tropaeolum speciosum*

AUTUMN INTEREST
- *Cotoneaster horizontalis*
- *Parthenocissus henryana*
- *Pyracantha rogersiana*
- *Vitis coignetiae* (grows very big so needs space)

West-facing walls

IN MANY WAYS A WEST-FACING WALL IS THE PERFECT PLACE TO GROW ALL BUT THE MOST TENDER PLANTS. It is shaded from the worst of the midday sun, yet protected from cold east and north winds. Any plant with a strong colour looks good on a west wall. By evening the light is carrying the accumulated heat of the day so that a west-facing wall will be much warmer than one facing east, and the light will be thicker and more intense. Strong colours seem to absorb this quality and reflect it, so that oranges, purples and deep crimsons look at their best against a west wall.

A west wind is often wet but usually warm, making a west-facing wall the only one that is likely to have anything like enough moisture from rain alone. Perhaps the best combination of climbing plants is that of roses and clematis, especially if the clematis uses the rose to twine through and flowers either before or after the rose. This extends the show, making it easier to justify giving precious space to some of the wonderful roses like 'Constance Spry' or, if you have a large wall, one of the less vigorous ramblers like 'Sanders' White', both of which flower for only about six weeks in midsummer. One of the late-flowering clematis, like those in the jackmannii group, or a *Clematis viticella* would take on where the roses left off and would be pruned back to allow the rose all the room it needed earlier in the season. Like roses, clematis like plenty of moisture at their roots and will be completely happy on a west wall.

A west wall is a perfect situation for apples and pears, and even peaches, figs and apricots should grow well and their fruit ripen. In many ways the hardest thing about a west-facing wall is knowing what *not* to grow, because in a small garden space is bound to be the limiting factor.

Wisteria sinensis needs the warmth of a west- or south-facing wall if it is to fully develop its long racemes of flower.

BEST PLANTS FOR WEST-FACING WALLS

EVERGREENS
Camellia japonica
Camellia x *williamsii* cultivars
Ceanothus (Californian lilac)
Escallonia 'Iveyi'
Magnolia

SPRING-FLOWERING
Camellia japonica
Camellia x *williamsii* cultivars
Ceanothus (Californian lilac)
Clematis armandii (evergreen)
Lonicera periclymenum 'Belgica' (early Dutch honeysuckle)

SUMMER-FLOWERING
All roses

AUTUMN-FLOWERING
Clematis viticella 'Mme Julia Correvon'
Lonicera periclymenum 'Serotina' (late Dutch honeysuckle)

WINTER-FLOWERING
Chimonanthus praecox (wintersweet)
Clematis cirrhosa var. *balearica*
Lonicera fragrantissima (winter-flowering honeysuckle)

WHITE-FLOWERED
Clematis 'Duchess of Edinburgh'

YELLOW-FLOWERED
Clematis 'Bill Mackenzie'
Rosa 'Allgold'

PINK-FLOWERED
Rosa 'Constance Spry'

BLUE-FLOWERED
Clematis 'Beauty of Worcester'

PURPLE/MAUVE-FLOWERED
Clematis 'Etoile Violette'
Clematis 'Royalty'

RED/ORANGE-FLOWERED
Clematis 'Niobe'
Eccremocarpus scaber (Chilean glory flower)

FRUITING
Any apple, pear, plum, cherry, or peach
Cydonia oblonga (quince)

ANNUAL
Lathyrus odoratus (sweet pea)
Lagenaria vulgaria (bottle gourd)

FAST-GROWING
Evergreen ceanothus
Clematis montana

GOOD SCENT
Clematis armandii
Jasminum officinale (summer jasmine)
Lonicera x *italica* (American honeysuckle)
Wisteria sinensis

Clematis viticella 'Alba Luxurians' is one of the many varieties of *Clematis viticella*, all of which flower in late summer and autumn.

Flowers

(ABOVE) Although the archetypal delphinium is blue, they actually come
in many colours and shades. This white one is 'Sandpiper'.
(RIGHT) A small back garden can still be packed with hundreds of flowers.

Growing flowers

MOST PEOPLE (with the exception of a few and often very interesting gardeners) expect flowers to be the showpiece of their gardens. In an ideal world we would have the place spilling over with colour, scent and exquisite form every week of the year. It can be done but I would suggest that it is best to accept some initial compromises. Ask yourself some questions: When are you going to be in the garden? What time of day and season of the year are you going to enjoy it most? Do you go away at all? How much work are you intending to put into it? What, in other people's gardens, have you most liked?

The last question may be the hardest if you do not know the name of any plants, but it is often a good starting point. The other answers will eliminate fruitless areas. When we lived in London my wife and I used to work seven days a week from August through to the end of March. Other than the late summer evenings, it meant that by the end of summer the garden was essentially over until spring. This in turn meant that spring and early summer flowers were especially important to us and we tried to have as wide a selection as possible. Looking at your own lifestyle, it may be that you go away most weekends, or for the entire month of August, or perhaps you only ever use the garden in the evenings. These factors will certainly affect your perception of the garden and should therefore influence your choice of flowers.

The next point is really the most important of all. Prepare your soil well and go on treating it as the most precious commodity in the garden. It is an absolute fact that the better your soil is in structure and richness, the more flowers you will have in the garden. 'Good' soil has a deep layer of topsoil with plenty of organic matter mixed into it, it drains well and yet holds moisture, it has no large stones in it and it is not heavy. It should smell and feel good. This is rare in nature and very rare indeed in a town, so you have to work at it, but 'bad' soil can be converted and over a few years any soil can be greatly improved.

However good your soil and however clever you are at growing flowers, you can still make the place look ugly. *What* you grow matters much more than how you grow it – a fact that very few garden writers or broadcasters seem to have cottoned onto. Nothing is viewed in isolation. Always consider the effect that flowers have upon each other. Two individually beautiful plants might not work well together. The overall effect should always take precedence over individual beauty, and the smaller your garden is, the less leeway you have. Be ruthless with any individual flower – however lovely – if it does not actively contribute to the broader appeal of the garden.

Introducing colour through flowers

THE VISUAL APPEAL OF A GARDEN IS MADE UP OF TEXTURE, FORM, SCENT AND, ABOVE ALL, COLOUR.

Books have been written on the use of colour in the garden, but here are a few points to think about:

- Never 'dot' colour about. Even in a small garden it is better to plant in confident blocks. If you like a flower, always buy at least three plants and make them into one group.

- Use colour as a surprise. Break the garden up so that you cannot see it all at once and treat the separate areas as different colour-schemes – exactly like different rooms inside the house. Work with the given qualities of each area so that the colour is seen to its best advantage.

- Light affects colour enormously. Pastel colours and whites always look best in gentle light, but are bleached out by midday sun. Purples, rich reds, oranges and deep blues look very good in low evening light. Yellow, blue and green can best withstand harsh midday light.

- Use the colour wheel. Colours that are close to each other are harmonious, while opposites intensify each other. So if you want to achieve a truly yellow effect you must include a small amount of blue or purple and to get the most vivid red it must be partnered with green.

- Some colours are much rarer than others in the plant world. There are fewer truly blue flowers than any other colour and white flowers are the most common. Both these colours, incidentally, do well in shade. Magenta and orange are vibrant and vital; they can clash horribly with pink though they are enriched and enriching with purple.

- Consider the seasonal succession of colour. You may have snowdrops followed by crocus, daffodils, tulips and then annuals, all in the same small area or container. Do not treat each group as a crop that has no relationship to the one that preceded or will follow it. Either keep to the same range of colour so that this becomes a fixed point of reference in the garden or relate the colours to what else is going on nearby at the same time.

- The neutral tones of the background are as important as the colours for which they provide infill. In practice this means foliage. Glaucous leaves, with a silvery sheen over a blue/green base, are very effective with pastel colours as well as lovely in their own right. Rich green leaves

The pink bedding dahlia 'Coltness Gem'.

tend to balance deep, intense colours; the most obvious example is holly. Purple leaves make a rich foil, but use them sparingly because they have a tendency to absorb light.

- Do not underestimate the depth and strength of green. It is the most powerful weapon in the colour arsenal as well as the most accommodating.

- Pink is a difficult colour and yet has a 'pretty' tag that makes people unthinkingly reach for it. On its own or with greys, shades of white, lemon, violet, or any chalky mix of colour it can look superb, and there is a huge range of pink flowers from which to choose. But richness and intensity is easily diluted and distracted by even a little pink. As ever, consider the overall effect rather than assessing the garden piecemeal.

- When colours jangle and tangle with each other they can achieve a gaudiness that is exhilarating and fun rather than just irritating. This is as difficult a balance to strike successfully in the garden as it is in the home, but it can be fun to try. The trick is to go for it with conviction, using the brightest tones available.

Annuals

ANNUALS ARE THE BEST FRIEND OF THE NEW GARDEN OR INEXPERIENCED GARDENER. While most perennials take two or three years to get into their stride and perhaps five to mature fully, annuals do their stuff gloriously fast. All you have to do is stick some seeds in the ground, make sure they are watered, thin them out a bit and let them get on with it. They are also the most economical way to fill a garden with colour. A cheap packet of seeds will produce dozens of healthy plants that will grow better than those bought in a tray. Some annuals, like poppies or annual lupins, dislike their roots being disturbed so *must* be sown where they are to flower.

Before you sow any seeds, prepare the ground thoroughly, mixing in as much compost or manure as you can get hold of. The speed of their growth means that most annuals need a lot of goodness to thrive. Rake the soil very fine. This is the best test to judge whether the time is right to sow them – if the soil is lumpy or feels cold to touch, then wait a few days and try again. There are no hard and fast rules – just trust your instincts.

One problem in growing annuals from seed is that the emerging seedlings can look remarkably like weeds. If you hoe them you will lose your flowers but if you don't they will be choked by the more vigorous weeds. The best way round this is to sow the seeds in zigzags, crosses or circles and stick a cane in the middle. You should be able to spot the difference as they emerge and by the time they are fully grown the plants will make attractive clumps and the patterns will not be noticeable. However carefully you sow, you *must* thin the seedlings as they emerge. This might seem disastrously wasteful of precious seedlings but be ruthless and leave a gap of at least 5-8cm (2-3in) between each plant to give them room for nutrients and space to grow.

WHAT IS AN ANNUAL?

ANNUALS germinate, mature, flower, set their seed and die in the same season. They are divided into two types:

Hardy annuals withstand frost but need plenty of light to grow and flower. They are best sown or planted in March or April and will flower until they have set all their seed. Dead-heading flowers as they fade will encourage them to keep on flowering for longer.

Opium poppies (*Papaver somniferum*), cornflowers (*Centaurea cyanus*), sweet peas (*Lathrous odoratus*) and corncockles (*Agrostemma*) are all hardy annuals.

Half-hardy annuals are frost-tender and should only be planted or sown after the middle of May. The first frosts of autumn will kill them.

Bells of Ireland (*Moluccella laevis*), sunflowers (*Helianthus annuus*), busy lizzies (*Impatiens*) and snapdragons (*Antirrhinum*) are all half-hardy annuals.

BIENNIALS establish leaves and roots the first season (summer) and flower and set seed the following spring or summer (although this may all happen within a 12-month period). They are best planted in September where you want them to flower the following spring. If you sow them, do so in a special seed bed and transplant them at the end of summer. Foxgloves (*Digitalis*), forget-me-nots (*Myosotis*), hollyhocks (*Alcea*), wallflowers (*Cheiranthus*) and sweet Williams (*Dianthus barbatus*) are examples of biennials.

GROWING FLOWERS FOR CUTTING

Annuals are also the best way to provide large bunches of cut flowers. Plan for this by:

- Making extra sure you feed them (to encourage vigorous plants with large flowers and long stems).

- Thinning them slightly less than normal initially, then cutting them selectively to thin them out further throughout the flowering season.

- Sowing two or three successive 'crops', starting in March and finishing at the end of May, to give a supply right through until the autumn.

The white foxglove *Digitalis purpurea* f. *albiflora* is a biennial ideal for dry shady corners, gleaming out of the shadows.

Spring annuals

SPRING IN BRITAIN MEANS MARCH, APRIL AND MAY. In theory there could be frost in any of these months although most town gardens are frost-free in May. This means that spring annuals have to be hardy, so do not waste time trying to grow half-hardy annuals until the second week of May. This limitation – as with all restrictions in gardening – can actually be helpful. It confines the choice of plants to a more manageable number and also means that you can orchestrate change and succession as spring turns into early summer.

Most hardy annuals should be sown in March and April and they start to flower from May onwards. This is the easiest way to produce flowers but it does not provide you with a display while they are getting established. To do that you need to start planning the year before by sowing biennials. That is great if you are sufficiently interested and organised, but if you forget, or just don't get round to it, it means buying plants (biennials) that have been grown from seed the previous summer and autumn. These are best bought by the tray from garden centres or – best of all – street markets, where they are often very good value.

The weather dictates exactly when and what appears first, but as I write this in the first week of March the pale blue flowers of **Forget-me-nots** (*Myosotis*) are starting to appear. Because these self-seed so voraciously it is easy to overlook their individual loveliness, with their tiny flowers that can shift from blue to mauve according to the cast of the light and their mouse-ear leaves. Although they carpet the ground indiscriminately, they are easy to dig up and thin out.

Wallflowers (*Cheiranthus cheiri*) can start to flower in February. They have a knack of seeding themselves in the cracks of paths or even walls (I know a castle in Wales where they flower every year 18m (50ft) up on the side of a tower). Their scent is spicy and warm – like dust after a sprinkle of rain on a hot day. They are strictly biennial and must be sown in May or June and planted, about 30cm (1ft) apart, where they are to flower in September. These will undoubtedly flower much better than plants purchased and planted in early spring.

The **double daisies** (*Bellis perennis*) are really perennials, but they are nearly always treated as an annual. They make very good low pink and red spring bedding, planted in March to flower through to summer. Like forget-me-nots, they make excellent partners to spring bulbs.

Sweet rocket (*Hesperis matronalis*) fills a big gap after most bulbs have finished and before much else begins. Butterflies adore it and so do I. The flowers are all pastel-coloured and grow about 1m (3ft) tall, filling the evening air with the scent of cloves. These, too, seed themselves like mad; if you like them this is a boon, and if for some obscure reason you do not, simply pull them up.

The flowers of **honesty** (*Lunaria annua*), ranging from white through to purple, look a bit like those of rocket. Honesty is really grown for the distinctive seedpods that shift from green pods resembling flattened peas to ghostly silver moons later in the year. It is biennial and seeds itself, and it can be dug up and moved, unlike most biennials which dislike disturbance.

The *Viola* 'Myfanwy' nestles amongst the grape hyacinth *Muscari* 'Azureum' in spring sunshine.

Summer annuals

IT IS SUMMER AND ALL ANNUALS ARE IN A HURRY. They have to get on and mature, flower, attract insects to pollinate them and set seeds. The long daylight hours and the warmth of summer represent their one opportunity and they take it gloriously. In a small garden you will be spoilt for choice, so be rigorous in working out what colours, heights and general effects you want. It is easy to lose a garden to its plants, which is why larger gardens benefit from being divided into a number of smaller spaces, each with an individual theme.

However you can if you wish use the range of plants available to cram your space to the full, especially by growing plants of varying heights, from out-and-out climbers to tiny little affairs.

ANNUAL CLIMBERS

Sweet peas (*Lathyrus odoratus*) are the best of all the annual climbers. There is no point in growing a sweet pea that does not smell sweetly, so avoid most modern varieties and stick to reliably scented plants like the Spencer group. Sweet peas grow very well up trellis, netting, or in a pot up a wigwam of canes. If planted at the base of a wall they will need lots of water. They also like the richest soil possible. If you keep picking the flowers they will bloom into October.

Black-eyed Susan (*Thunbergia alata*) will grow to 3m (10ft) and has striking yellow or orange flowers with chocolate centres (yum!).

TALL ANNUALS

Tall-growing annuals can be very useful at the back of a border to stagger the height of flowering. But any annual growing over 1.2m (4ft) will need some kind of support.

Hollyhocks (*Alcea rosea*) will reach 2.5m (8ft) and are excellent for giving a soft, cottage-garden feel.

Sunflowers (*Helianthus annuus*) are not all giants and not all sunny yellow. 'Velvet Queen' is a glorious russet and 'Lemon Queen' is, er, lemon. Both grow to about 1.5m (5ft).

Flowering tobacco (*Nicotiana sylvestris*) has my favourite scent of all plants and grows to 1.2–1.5m (4–5ft).

Cosmos (*C. bipinnatus*) is a tall, delicately branched plant with beautifully elegant flowers; try the white 'Purity'.

SCENTED ANNUALS

Because they are so desperate for pollination, scent is often an important part of the annual's armoury. Use it!

In addition to *Nicotiania sylvestris* (see above), my favourite scented annuals include: *Cosmos atrosanguineus* (chocolate-scented), lemon verbena (*Lippia citriodora*), night-scented stock (*Matthiola incana*) with a warm, spicy scent and evening primrose (*Oenothera biennis*), whose fragrance, like that of tobacco plants, is much stronger at night.

ANNUALS FOR SHADE

Although most annuals need as much sun as possible, some have adapted to grow in shade. My favourite is the **white foxglove** (*Digitalis purpurea f. albiflora*) which will grow gracefully in almost complete shade and, like night-scented stock, even in dry shade, which is rare. **Tobacco plants** all grow in shade (but do not necessarily prefer it) and the **monkey flower** (*Mimulus*), is completely happy without direct light. **Evening primrose** grows anywhere with some moisture or heavy soil – it seeds very freely.

The important thing is to keep your eyes open, to note what you like and find out their names. Discriminate. Garden centres only sell plants that are easy to grow and store. Hunt out the plants you want. In addition to the annuals listed above, I also love the following:

- *Anthemis tinctoria* (marguerites)

- *Argyranthemum* (especially *A.* 'Jamaica Primrose')

- *Brachycome iberidifolia* (Swan River daisy)

- *Calendula officinalis* (marigolds)

- *Centaurea cyanus* (cornflowers)

- *Eschscholzia californica* (Californian poppies)

- *Limnanthes douglasii* (poached-egg plant)

- *Moluccella laevis* (Irish bells)

- *Nigella damascena* (love-in-a-mist)

- *Papaver* (poppies)

- *Tagetes erecta* (African marigolds)

- *Tithonia rotundifolia*

- *Tropaeolum* (nasturtiums)

The biggest of all annuals is the sunflower *Helianthus annuus*, reaching up to 5m (16ft) tall by late summer.

Autumn annuals

SOME ANNUALS LINGER ON WELL INTO AUTUMN, OTHERS CREEP IN THERE BY DEFAULT, AS A RESULT OF A LATE SUMMER. Either way, they are very welcome because, unlike the giddy days of high summer, the garden is running out of flowers. To extend the season of annuals it is important to keep dead-heading the flowers and to pick as many as possible for the house. They will respond by making new flowers in a desperate effort to reproduce.

Rudbeckias are excellent flowers for late summer into autumn, with *R. hirta* among the easiest to grow. They have yellow and golden flowers with dark centres; try 'Rustic Dwarfs' or 'Goldilocks'. Likewise *Bidens ferulifolia*, which has fern-like foliage and all yellow flowers. Both are variations on the daisy, both come from America and both perform well.

Marigolds are always one of the longest-lasting annuals, flowering strongly until the first hard frosts. The African marigolds (*Tagetes erecta*) and the French marigold (*Tagetes patula*) are neither African nor French, both of them coming from Mexico. African marigolds are larger than the French ones and do not have the latter's unpleasant smell (although modern varieties smell fine). French marigolds flower faster than almost any other garden plant, budding within a few weeks of sowing. They are compact and make good subjects for window boxes and containers. But I prefer the African ones, which seem to have more vitality and louche charm. Both types like sun and good drainage.

In my garden the **nasturtiums** take over great swathes of ground by autumn. I let them do this because they are fun, but in a smaller garden they can easily be controlled simply by hacking them back – which will do them no harm. The first proper frosts will kill them, but until then they flower rampantly and are a happy reminder of the exuberance of summer.

Pansies (*Viola* x *wittrockiana*) are really perennials but should be treated as annuals or biennials as they flower much better in their first year. However, they will go on flowering into winter, although they should be dead-headed to allow the plant to have a rest and build up strength before spring. 'Jackanapes' is a very old variety and as pretty as any, with its yellow and russet flowers. 'Bowles' Black' sounds sombre but is in fact elegant and lovely and very long-flowering if picked regularly; it is particularly attractive and long-lasting as a cut flower.

SPRING ANNUALS TO SOW IN AUTUMN

Some annuals are sufficiently hardy to be sown in autumn and in consequence will have a headstart the following spring. These include:

- *Centaurea cyanus* (cornflowers)

- *Myosotis* (forget-me-nots)

- *Nemophila*

- *Nigella damascena* (love-in-a-mist)

- *Phacelia*

- *Papaver* (poppies)

The annual nasturtium, *Tropaeolum*, will flower gaudily until the first hard frosts, sometimes swamping other plants.

Bulbs

WHAT DIFFERENTIATES A BULB FROM ANY OTHER TYPE OF PLANT IS THAT THE NOURISHMENT FOR THE FLOWER IS ALL STORED WITHIN THE BULB ITSELF. This is why a bulb will begin to shoot while still unplanted. It is an amazing little time bomb, with not only the nourishment but all the memory needed to tell the shoot how big to grow and when to flower stored within that dry little root.

When a bulb has finished blooming, its leaves are greedily converting sunlight and water into the nourishment for next year's flower and they – the leaves – feed from the bulb's roots. That is why you must never cut off the leaves from a bulb after it has flowered. Allow for this period of die-back when you plant bulbs by planting something in front of, or around, them, or planting bulbs under shrubs which will come into leaf as they finish flowering. You do not want the garden ruined for weeks by yellowing, dying leaves and yet it is important to leave them until they die back of their own accord before tidying them up – or you may find that there will not be enough food stored and the plant will be 'blind' in a year's time.

Of all garden flowers, bulbs are the ones that require the most planning. With the exception of snowdrops, which can be planted very successfully when still in flower, by the time you notice the flowers and think that you would like some in your garden, you are already a year too late. Remember:

- Bulbs that flower from Christmas to May must be planted in early autumn; tulips are best planted in November.
- Bulbs that flower between June and November should be planted in early spring.

A lot of bulbs are planted too shallow, whereas it will do them no harm to be planted too deep. Allow at least twice their own depth of soil above them and put them pointed-end up. In principle, nothing could be easier. However, in practice, the ground is often like rock and the dibber (pointed stick) won't dib a proper hole and I find bulb planting a very boring job. But the results are worth being bored for an hour or two each year. A bulb planter, which removes a plug of soil that you can put back over the planted bulb, makes life easier, but if your soil is heavy it is a good idea to put a handful of grit or sharp sand into each hole as few bulbs react well to sitting in the wet. In an ideal world – the world of gardening books – you should add a small handful of bonemeal too. Bonemeal is an ideal feed as it provides the minerals (potash and phosphate) needed to make flowers and strong roots but not too much nitrogen, which would only stimulate lush leaves.

A BULB BY ANY OTHER NAME

We tend to call anything that is bulbous a 'bulb', whereas there are a number of bulbous roots that have different characteristics.

- **BULBS** are made from concentric layers of fleshy leaves with a protective dry outer layer: **daffodils** and **tulips** are typical examples. However, some lilies and fritillaries have no protective skin and the scales are separate.

- **CORMS,** made from the swollen base of the stem, are replaced by new corms every year. **Crocuses, gladioli** and **colchicums** are all corms.

- **TUBERS** are the swollen roots that are used for food storage – unlike most roots which are solely a medium for conveying food to the plant. Tubers are found in **dahlias, anemones** and in some **orchids.**

- **RHIZOMES** are swollen underground, usually horizontal stems, and the best known examples are **irises** and **lily-of-the-valley.**

Spring bulbs

THE MAJORITY OF SPRING BULBS COME FROM MOUNTAINOUS, almost alpine conditions, which means they have a very short growing season between winter and summer. Most enjoy a summer baking, are very well drained, yet get plenty of water from melting snow in spring. Consequently cold is rarely a problem but too much dampness can be.

It may be hard to replicate the average alpine scree slope in the middle of a sodden city garden but some bulbs, like snowdrops and fritillaries, are well suited to damp and some grit or sharp sand placed in the hole underneath the bulb when you plant it works pretty well. Another way of growing bulbs that prefer dry conditions – such as crocus, daffodils, tulips and scillas – in ground that is fundamentally wet is to plant them around the roots of a deciduous tree or shrub which will take up most of the available moisture in the ground.

PLANTING BULBS

Of course spring bulbs look great in a border before any of the perennials or annuals have started to flower. When you are planting a border from scratch, you should plant your bulbs after you have put in the shrubs and herbaceous plants, even if that means leaving it very late, otherwise you will dig them up when the rest of the border gets planted. Whenever you plant them it is important to go deep. In general, the bigger the bulb the deeper it can go, with tulips quite happy buried with 25cm (10in) of soil above them. All bulbs want to be at least deep enough for you to be able to plant small annuals over the top of them.

Bulbs always look better in groups than singly and it is preferable to plant bulbs thickly in a pot than to spread them thinly around a border. Try and plant bulbs as soon after buying them as possible, as they grow much better when 'fresh'. As a rough guide, I would say that no small bulb (like crocus, snowdrop, muscari, scilla) should ever be less than 8cm (3in) from another and no big one (daffodils, tulips, trilliums) more than 23cm (9in). The secret of planting in grass is to take handfuls of

bulbs and throw them roughly where you want them to appear, and then plant them where they land. This is far more effective in achieving a naturalistic look than the plodding eye can ever be. Once the flowers are over, you must not cut the grass until the leaves of the bulbs have started to yellow and die down.

While there is room in every garden for scillas, fritillaries, aconites, anemones, iris and muscari, the four major spring bulbs are snowdrops, crocus, daffodils and tulips, and a small selection of each will provide flower from January through to mid-May. I love bluebells, especially when they carpet a wood as far as the eye can see, but they are very invasive once they get established and can become a major weed. In a small garden it is better to grow them in containers.

Two very contrasting bulbs. Tiny snowdrops (LEFT) are amongst the first and best of all bulbs and will happily grow in damp shade.
The yellow Crown imperial fritillary *Fritillaria imperialis* 'Lutea' (ABOVE) will reach 1.5m (5ft) tall, flowering in April and May.

Spring bulbs

SNOWDROPS

For most people a snowdrop is a snowdrop but there are actually 350 species and cultivars to choose from, if that is your bent. You may find that dry bulbs planted laboriously but horticulturally correctly produces a disappointing crop of flowers. Try and buy them 'in the green' and plant them from January through to March; they will then flower for you to the best of their ability. Snowdrops will grow well in shade which adds usefulness to their beauty. All snowdrops should be planted in clumps, either to spread in large drifts composed of small clumps on open grass, or among trees, shrubs and perennial plants – again in small groups. It is important to get the size of these groups right and that can only be judged by eye: too big and they become anonymous and too small and they look naked and abandoned. Increase the spread by digging snowdrops up after flowering and before the leaves die back, splitting the clump into two or three and replanting separately.

CROCUS

There are over 80 species of crocus but they all come in only three colours – purple, yellow and white. Crocus do best on well-drained soil where they get full midday sun and should be planted accordingly. We grow them in shallow terracotta bulb pans and bring them indoors when they start to flower. They can be put outside for the rest of the year once the flowering is done. Crocuses are better than daffodils for planting in grass that is to be mown, as their leaves take less time to die back and therefore will not delay mowing.

DAFFODILS

I think that daffodils are difficult to grow in a small garden. They look great in huge swathes but slightly ridiculous dotted about in a border. Plant them in clumps around trees and shrubs or in larger groups in a border. Avoid mixing different species and cultivars, but keep to strong groups. When planting in grass it is curiously difficult to avoid planting in a system or pattern and thereby spoiling the attempt at a natural look. The leaves should not be cut, or tied into absurd knots, until they are completely brown or at least six weeks after the last flower. This is usually towards the end of June, by which time they have definitely outstayed their welcome.

A window box planted as thickly as possible with daffodils looks great and these bulbs always look fine in pots as long as they are crammed in, daffodil cheek to daffodil jowl. When they have finished flowering the pots can be tucked away somewhere unobtrusive (but with some sunshine) until the leaves have died back.

TULIPS

Tulips have inspired intense passions since their introduction to the west in the seventeenth century. Hardly any plant is so opulent, sensual or blatantly rich and time invested on tulips reaps a brash, publicly measurable reward. You do not need – or want – to plant tulips in blocks – leave that to the municipal parks department. Use their intensity of colour to create ribbons within a border or plant them in small groups where their brightness is intensified by the green of foliage around them. They must have good drainage and sunshine, so put plenty of grit beneath each bulb and, if in pots, add perlite (which can be bought in bags at a garden centre) to the compost and make sure the pot is raised off the ground so that it can drain properly.

(RIGHT) Portrait of the white snakeshead fritillary, *Fritillaria* 'Alba'.

Spring bulbs for damp soil

- *Anemone blanda* (wood anemones)

- *Eranthis hyemalis* (aconites)

- *Fritillaria*

- *Galanthus nivalis* (snowdrops)

- *Hyacinthoides non-scriptus* (bluebells)

- *Leucojum aestivum* (summer snowflakes)

- *Narcissus cyclamineus*

- *Tulipa sylvestris*

Summer and autumn bulbs

IT IS A PITY TO LIMIT YOUR CHOICE OF BULBS TO THOSE THAT FLOWER IN SPRING. Lilies, iris, alliums, dahlias and gladioli are all bulbous plants and there is a small group of autumn-flowering bulbs, like nerines and cyclamen, that deserve wider recognition. The time to plant summer and autumn bulbs is in spring, around the time that daffodils and tulips are flowering. But a good guide is their availability at garden centres and shops – if the bulbs are for sale, then it is a good time to plant them.

LILIES

Lilies are the divas of the garden and although they have a reputation for being tricky to grow (and some certainly are), there are equally some that are very easy and which add fabulous glamour to a garden.

The lily family includes red-hot pokers (*Kniphofia*) and autumn crocus (*Colchicum*), although it does not include lily-of-the-valley or day lilies. But to follow genealogical accuracy is to miss the point. For the true lily-experience, you need the *Lilium* species and its hybrids alone.

Lilium regale is one of the easiest as well as one of the best lilies, with up to 10 deliciously scented, funnel-shaped white flowers. It will grow up to 2m (6ft) tall so it needs staking; if grown in a container, make sure that the pot is substantial enough to provide ballast for it when fully grown. *Lilium henryi* has over a dozen orange flowers per stem. The Madonna lily (*Lilium candidum*) is unusual in that it will grow in limy soil and needs to be planted shallowly, with only 2.5cm (1in) of soil covering it. It is best planted in late summer as it starts to grow in winter and flowers first of all the lilies, in late spring.

Lily bulbs have no protective layer, so they are very susceptible to drying out both before and after planting. Keep bulbs covered until you plant them and make sure they get plenty of water as they grow.

ALLIUMS

Alliums are dramatic members of the onion family grown for their spherical flowerheads (although any vegetable gardener will know that leeks allowed to go to seed are as decorative as any flower). All alliums like a well-drained, sunny position and should keep flowering for years if left undisturbed.

Allium aflatunense is very easy to grow, with a pompom of purple flowers on a straight stem up to 1m (3ft) tall in early summer. *A. flavum* has yellow heads and *A.* 'Purple Sensation' great purple globes.

CROCOSMIA

Crocosmia has nothing to do with crocus and everything to do with a really good, powerful summer flower accompanied by grass-like spears of leaf. *Crocosmia* 'Lucifer' is striking for its intense scarlet flowers. It is dead easy to grow.

DAHLIAS

Dahlias belong to a very old-fashioned world of gardening but many of them are making thoroughly modern and brilliant additions to the late summer border. There are hundreds of varieties, but avoid the lipstick-lurid pinks, oranges and yellows and go for the truly intense colours, especially the scarlets and ruby reds, that can be obtained. Dahlias are less straightforward to

The superb pink globes of *Allium aflatunense* dominate a summer border.

grow since they are frost-tender and need very rich soil: plant them out 15cm (6in) deep in April. Cut the stems back a few inches before digging them up after the first frosts. They should be stored somewhere cool, dry and frost-free over winter.

GLADIOLI
After Dame Edna, it is hard to take gladioli seriously, but they can add presence and colour as autumn approaches. Like dahlias, you should avoid the hideous colours they can come in and stick to either the rich colours or the very pale yellows and pure white. Lift the corms at the same time as dahlia tubers.

COLCHICUMS AND CYCLAMEN
At the same time as the gladioli are flowering, colchicums are much more modestly appearing from the ground, the flowers preceding the leaves. They should be planted in the lee of a wall or shrub as they are very prone to wind damage, although *Colchicum speciosum* is fairly weather-resistant. The flowers of colchicums resemble spring crocuses – until the leaves, which are much broader, appear. *Crocus speciosus* is a crocus and looks like one; it just flowers in autumn. *Cyclamen hederifolium* look similar to large violets and, if given time to spread, are delicately beautiful around a small shady tree in October. They like very dry soil so do well around water-greedy tree roots; plant them very shallow.

Perennials

A PERENNIAL IS A PLANT THAT LIVES FOR AT LEAST TWO YEARS and an herbaceous perennial produces all its leaves, flowers and seeds between spring and summer. It then effectively hibernates throughout winter, continuing to live underground as all the top growth dies right back to the soil. This is to protect their leaves – which, unlike the tough woody stems of a shrub or tree, are soft and full of moisture – from the cold. In spring, as the ground warms up and the daylight lengthens, the new leaves push through again. In order to sustain this annual sprint to full growth, the roots tend to be substantial and will increase in size from year to year. There are a few evergreen perennials, such as hellebores, ajuga and some euphorbias, and these are especially useful in winter.

Perennials exist for every conceivable type of soil and situation and they can be grown all together – as in a proper herbaceous border – or else mixed in with shrubs, bulbs and annuals to make a mixed border. In short, they are an integral part of any garden. They are also very easy to move about in their dormant period until you find exactly the right spot for them, which makes them thoroughly accommodating plants.

PLANTING PERENNIALS

I shall look at the possibilities for using perennials throughout the year in the following pages, but there are general points about planting them that apply to all gardens in all seasons.

I PLANT IN GROUPS

Resist the understandable temptation to spread your relatively expensive perennials around the available space. They look much better in clumps of three or five plants. If you buy large plants it is often a good idea to divide them immediately into two or three and plant them as a group rather than a single plant. This way they will grow faster and more healthily. The obvious conclusion to this policy in a small garden is severely to restrict your choice of plants and to make the ones you do have room for seem abundant and really spectacular.

(ABOVE) A group of *Verbascum bombyciferum* planted close together makes an effective drift in a border.

(RIGHT) *Echinops ritro* just before the flowers open shows why it is called the globe thistle. A really good structural addition to any border.

2 PERENNIALS ARE HUNGRY

They need deep, rich soil and lots of goodness added regularly. Traditionally the plants were lifted every three years or so and the border completely redug, but this is now thought to be unnecessary. Simply mulch the border each spring with a thick layer of rotted manure or compost. What remains as essential today as it was a hundred years ago, is to prepare the ground really well for perennials. Dig it deeply and add as large a quantity of organic material as you can lay your hands on. The difference between average and really spectacular gardens lies as much in the quality of the soil as in the plants that grow in it.

3 SUPPORT YOUR PLANTS

And support them *before* they need it, not afterwards, when the damage has been done. Perennials have masses of soft growth and tend to be top-heavy. In their natural setting it does not matter if they get bashed about as long as they set seed, but this spoils them for the garden. Ideally you want to get the support around the bottom half of the plant so that it is hidden by subsequent growth.

You can use short canes and soft twine (soft, so that it does not damage the delicate new growth), otherwise you can use longer canes and then tie the plants to them as they grow.

Spring perennials

SPRING DELIVERS TWO TYPES OF PERFORMANCE FROM PERENNIALS. The first is ubiquitous, regardless of type, as the new leaves burst from the bare soil and you have an incredible array of fresh green foliage. The second is the flowering of early perennials. These are never rich swathes of colour but are inclined towards brilliant touches and delicate, light-filled washes of colour. The group of spring-flowering perennials is small and tends to be plants from deciduous woodland that need to flower and set seed before the leaf canopy blocks out too much light. They are therefore very suitable for growing among shrubs and trees and are ideal for a small garden.

If you collect your autumnal leaves and let them rot down over winter into a sweet-smelling, rich, crumbly leafmould (and you should do), these plants are the ideal recipients of its nourishing goodness.

MY FAVOURITE SPRING PERENNIALS

AQUILEGIA (COLUMBINE)
These spurred bell-flowers come in many colours and forms, notably the best shades of violet.

CORYDALIS FLEXUOSA
Has glaucous leaves and stunning delicate blue flowers that are both pale and deeply intense; likes moist shade.

DICENTRA SPECTABILIS (BLEEDING HEART)
Little pink, heart-shaped flowers hanging in a row from arching stems; 'Alba' is the white form.

EUPHORBIA
Especially E. characias and E. polychroma.

PAEONIA LACTIFLORA
Fabulously voluptuous flowers; plant shallowly.

PAPAVER ORIENTALIS (ORIENTAL POPPIES)
These flower briefly and gloriously in May, although their hairy leaves begin to grow as early as February. Untidy, sprawling and short-lived, they are still spectacular.

POLYGONATUM X HYBRIDUM (SOLOMON'S SEAL)
Resembles a cross between a dicentra and a hosta: pure white flowers like drops of milk hang off gracefully arching leaves; likes shade.

PRIMULA VULGARIS (PRIMROSE)
The wild primrose – so much lovelier than any of the hundreds of bred varieties.

PULMONARIA (LUNGWORT)
Can be a bit insipid, but 'Mawson's Blue' is very strong and pure.

VIOLA
The tiny, delicate flowers are exquisite.

TASKS FOR SPRING

Early spring is the best time to sort out your flower borders.

1   Cut away the dried tops of last year's growth and remove all dead foliage.

2   Any perennials that have become too big should be dug up and split. The best way to do this varies according to root type, but a sharp spade is usually the best tool for woody roots and fingers or a fork best for fibrous roots. Use the divided plant to create new groups, which will grow with renewed vigour. If you have very old plants, keep only the roots from the outside of the clump and ditch the middle part.

3   Weed thoroughly around all plants and mulch thickly with organic compost. If a perennial has weeds like couch grass, ground elder or bindweed growing among its roots, dig the whole plant up and wash the roots under a tap to remove the soil. Pick out and burn or bin every last piece of weed root, then replant the perennial.

Corydalis flexuosa has the most astonishingly china blue flowers of any plant. It thrives in light shade.

Summer perennials

SUMMER IS THE SEASON OF PERENNIALS. Because they grow so fast, they have a lushness and a blowsy quality that no other type of plant can match. Perennials tend to give good value in terms of longevity of flowering, with the first two months retaining freshness and a degree of delicacy, while by midsummer the tone of the garden is changing. The bigger perennials that have spent the previous few months concentrating on growing, begin to come into flower. Even in a small garden it is worth having some of these large plants as they will give a feeling of abundance and make the garden seem more spacious. But remember to grow them in clumps, not dotted about. Late summer is inevitably drier and the first wave of summer plants are past their best, with a second rank taking over.

MY FAVOURITE EARLY-SUMMER PERENNIALS

ACANTHUS (A. SPINOSA AND A. MOLLIS) (BEAR'S BREECHES)
Both species are great, with evergreen shiny leaves and spikes of white and purple flowers; will take almost total drought and will tolerate shade.

ALCHEMILLA MOLLIS (LADY'S MANTLE)
Will grow in deep shade; always has great charm, wherever it is grown; spreads very easily.

ANCHUSA AZUREA 'LODDON ROYALIST'
The best blue in the garden; can be short-lived.

DELPHINIUM
Must be as large as possible; dwarf delphiniums are a contradiction in terms.

TASKS FOR SUMMER

1 The main job in early summer is to make sure that your plants are really well supported.

2 If your soil is rich and well mulched, your perennials will not need watering, otherwise give them a good soak at their base once a week.

3 Dead-head plants as they fade to delay seeding and stimulate the production of more flowers.

GERANIUM
Not the clumsy pelargoniums, but the species geraniums, growing as ground cover with a mass of long-lasting and lovely little flowers ranging from pure white to near black.

GEUM (AVENS)
No other flower seems to last so well as the vermilion G. 'Mrs Bradshaw'.

HOSTA
I love the blue-leaved species best, of which *H. sieboldiana* is the most common. Mulch with grit to stop slugs and snails which unfortunately also love hostas.

BEARDED IRIS
Huge range of flowers, all with velvety, intense petals, and sword-shaped leaves.

The violent contrast of pink oriental poppies against lime foliage is loaded with spring sunshine.

MY FAVOURITE LATE-SUMMER PERENNIALS

ANEMONE x *HYBRIDA*
The Japanese anemones are long-lasting and reliably beautiful.

ECHINOPS RITRO (GLOBE THISTLE)
I love all thistles, but this is as good as any, with perfectly round purple flowers.

INULA HOOKERI
Sunburst-yellow daisy, like a broken umbrella growing 1.5m (5ft) tall; likes damp soil.

LIGULARIA STENOCEPHALA 'THE ROCKET'
Flames of yellow flower on black stems 1.5m (5ft) tall, shooting out from a clump of large toothed leaves; likes damp.

MACLEAYA MICROCARPA (PLUME POPPY)
Tall, feathery plumes of flower but the chalky blue/green leaves are the best thing about this plant: fantastic.

MONARDA 'CAMBRIDGE SCARLET'
As bright a vermilion as is available in plant form, but splashed against a strong backdrop of leaf so not at all overpowering.

NEPETA SIBIRICA (CATMINT)
The blue flowers last a long time and attract bees.

PENSTEMON
There are loads of penstemons but *P.* 'Garnet' is my favourite.

RUDBECKIA HIRTA (CONEFLOWER)
Another daisy, but more robust in appearance.

SALVIA PATENS
Pale blue flowers; needs full sun to do its best.

Autumn perennials

LATE SUMMER AND AUTUMN MERGE INTO EACH OTHER WITH A SLY INEVITABILITY. One minute it is the summer holidays and the next the back-to-school sadness of September, although early autumn can have some of the warmest and loveliest days of the year, with cool evenings and nights. For sheer colour, this is the best time of year for the garden. The parched, faded feel every garden suffers from in late summer is replaced by a fragile realisation that time is short. Despite the gentle dying of the leaves, plants take on a certain vigour in their final flourish before winter. Avoid the temptation to tidy borders too much in autumn – enjoy their slow and stylish decay.

There are few perennials that choose to begin their flowering in autumn, but those that do have a distinct leaning towards shades of purple in their colouring. This goes very well with the yellowing of foliage and the golden light that is characteristic of autumn.

My favourite autumn perennials

Aconitum (monkshood)

Flowers tend to be blue although it is available in yellows and ivories. 'Bressingham Spire' is just that – a spire of rich violet flowers. *A. japonicum* is very late-flowering. All have a dense mass of deeply cut leaves.

Aster (Michaelmas daisy)

There are scores of varieties to choose from, although I like the white ones such as *Aster novi-belgii* 'Schneckissen' or *A. novi-belgii* 'Monte Casino'. Avoid *A. novae-anglicae* as they spread very fast and go bald in the middle of the clump.

Cimicifuga simplex 'Elstead'

Soft white 'bottlebrush' flowers on long, dark stems; likes moist, leafy soils and some shade.

Gentiana

A number of gentians flower in early autumn. *G. septemfida* has beautifully intense blue flowers on floppy stems; needs sunshine.

Helenium 'Wyndley' and H. 'Moerheim Beauty'

H. 'Wyndley' has yellow flowers streaked with red like a russet shuttlecock whereas *H.* 'Moerheim Beauty' is almost brown; both are easy to grow.

Kniphofia

Many of these torch lilies get huge, but 'Little Maid' is compact enough for a small garden and has ivory spikes of flower in autumn. The standard red-hot poker (*K. triangularis*), is more conventionally red and grows to about 1m (3ft).

Melianthus major

This could have been included at any point in the growing season for its wonderful glaucous leaves, but it flowers (with a blood-red but unimportant fluorescence) in autumn – which would be spring in its native S. Africa – and is at its tallest then. It is tender, so give it your most sheltered spot and cut it to the ground after the first frost, then mulch the root. It will grow back to 1.2m (4ft) or more next year. A top plant.

Ophiopogon planiscapus 'Nigrescens'

This is grown for its black, grass-like leaves but it has pinky/mauve flowers in autumn; likes shade and fibrous soil.

Sedum spectabile

I could have chosen sedum in spring for their fat, smoky green leaves, summer for the pinkish flowers that attract bees and butterflies so voraciously, but autumn is really their season as they change colour. Robust, reliable and beautiful. Try 'Vera Jameson', which has purple leaves.

Verbena bonariensis

This is a winner. It has tall, square stems and purple clusters of flower that go right into winter; seeds everywhere and long may it do so.

(LEFT) *Sedum spectabile* is one of the few utterly reliable perennials of the garden, but it comes into its own in autumn until a hard frost knocks it back. It is particularly popular with butterflies.

Winter perennials

TRADITIONAL WISDOM has it that you should tidy perennials in winter, cutting back all dead growth and moving and dividing them as well as generally housekeeping the border. Do not do this: too much tidiness stifles the creative spirit and turns gardening into outdoor housework. There are also practical reasons for leaving perennials to die at theirown rate over winter. Firstly, cutting off dead growth removes all the seeds that would otherwise provide food for birds and, secondly, you lose the skeletal beauty of the winter garden. Finally, the dying top growth provides an insulating layer against the worst of the weather. The time to clear up is in March, when the new shoots are appearing.

The deadest time of the year in any northern-hemisphere garden is December and I have cheated slightly by including February and March in my winter calendar, whereas many people would class these months as early spring. In my defence, these two months often have the harshest weather of the year.

MY FAVOURITE WINTER PERENNIALS

ADONIS VERNALIS
Has golden-yellow flowers against ferny leaves. Likes a well-drained spot; mulch with gravel to deter slugs.

BERGENIA X SCHMIDTII
This is one of those plants that would probably not get selected if there was more to choose from: but it is worth having in the absence of competition. Has big, leathery leaves and clusters of pink flowers.

BRUNNERA MACROPHYLLA
Very good ground cover for an exposed position, flowering in late winter with forget-me-not flowers above heart-shaped leaves.

HELLEBORUS FOETIDUS
The easiest of all the hellebores to grow, this one is ideal for very dry shade. It has lovely crimson-rimmed flowers and finely cut leaves; plant in groups.

(ABOVE) *Brunnera macrophylla* is a woodland plant liking cool conditions, so ideal for providing colour early in the year in a shady spot.

(LEFT) The Lenton rose, *Helleborus orientalis,* is one of my favourite plants of all. It comes in colours ranging from almost pure white through pink to almost black, and has the most sensuously sumptuous flowers conceivable. And it flowers from February through to April. What more could one ask from a plant?

HELLEBORUS ORIENTALIS (LENTEN ROSE)

If there was one winter-flowering plant I had to choose above all others it would be this. It will flower from January to April and the flowers come in colours ranging from pure white to a purple so deep it is almost black, and each individual flower is often exquisitely marked on the inside of the petals. It needs really rich soil and some shade but is otherwise undemanding and will grow in almost total shade as long as it is not too dry. As it has very deep roots it dislikes being moved, but will grow well in a pot. Essential for every garden.

IRIS UNGUICULARIS

Will sometimes flower before Christmas and is stunningly unseasonal in its richness of colour. Short and delicate, it is worth growing if you have a hot spot where the roots can bake in summer. Hates being moved.

PULMONARIA RUBRA

An early pulmonaria with pink flowers; likes chalk.

Shrubs

A SHRUB DIFFERS FROM A TREE IN THAT IT DOES NOT HAVE A SINGLE STEM OR TRUNK AND FROM A PERENNIAL IN THAT ITS GROWTH IS WOODY OR HARDENED. New growth comes from buds along the stems. The range in size is enormous, from tiny heathers to huge rhododendrons and in appearance, from the vast blooms of magnolia and camellias to the clusters of tiny flowers on a forsythia or a pyracantha. Shrubs combine the permanence and bulk of trees with the flowers and speed of growth of perennials. This versatility and the fact that many of them need no attention at all once planted accounts for their rise in popularity over the last few decades.

Shrubs must be used carefully in a small garden. Like every single plant you have, they must be chosen with ruthless discrimination and positioned with meticulous attention to the overall needs of the garden, using them in conjunction with other plants to make the most of your space and their growing habits. For example, many deciduous shrubs offer perfect support for late-flowering clematis and provide exactly the right kind of dappled shade for spring bulbs and woodland flowers like primroses and violets. Evergreen shrubs tend to be more structural and architectural (see pages 38–39) although some of them do flower gorgeously. The shade they cast is usually too heavy and constant and their mass too dense for them to be part of integrated planting in the same way that a deciduous shrub can, and should, be. Thus, if you underplanted a deciduous shrub like *Viburnum plicatum* with snowdrops, scillas, daffodils and tulips, the bulbs would flower while the shrub slowly developed leaves in spring, and would then be hidden while their own leaves died back. The viburnum would flower in June, and a *Clematis jackmannii* could use its support to scramble up it, flowering in July and August. Thus in a tiny cameo you are creating a three-dimensional moving picture that changes every week of the year.

PLANTING SHRUBS

Shrubs need exactly the same treatment as a tree (see page 48). Dig a hole at least twice the size of the pot in which you bought the shrub. Remove the topsoil and loosen the subsoil thoroughly to the depth of a fork. Add plenty of compost and mix it in, then lower the shrub into the planting hole. Carefully mix topsoil round the roots, making sure that it is firmly heeled down so it will not be moved by the wind. I always plant shrubs in a slight saucer-like depression to hold water. Give it a large bucket or watering can full of water after planting. This obviously gives it liquid but also works the soil into any air pockets around the roots, which is important.

(ABOVE RIGHT) The tiers of *Vibernum plicatum* in spring. In autumn the leaves colour to a deep burnt red.

PRUNING SHRUBS

I know that people can be very anxious about pruning but if you follow these basic rules you will not go far wrong.

1 If in any doubt – do nothing. This will do no harm and will buy you time while you observe the next two rules.

2 Notice when the shrub flowers. As a very general rule, anything that flowers before June should be pruned immediately after flowering, as the new growth made in the remainder of the year will produce next year's flowers. A shrub that flowers in late summer makes its flowers on new growth and should be pruned in spring, which will encourage healthy new shoots to develop.

3 The harder you cut a shrub back in winter, the more vigorously it will regrow the following spring. If you want to prune something to restrict its size, do so in summer.

4 Always cut to *something* – be it a bud, a leaf, the ground or a fork in the branches.

Spring shrubs

SPRING IS REALLY TWO SEASONS IN THE GARDEN. From the middle of March to May it is a season of growth and activity and from the middle of April until June it is a celebration and a flowering season in its own right. Like all the first flowers of spring, the early shrubs shine singly, rather than as a massed effect. Their flowers are picked out against the generally barren background and, like winter-flowering shrubs, tend to be small and borne on leafless branches. By mid-spring flowers are starting to follow the leaves and create a much fuller, more sensuous effect. This tends to happen at the same time as blossom appears on the trees, so there is a total transformation of the garden and general excitement all round. You want a piece of that action in your garden.

Try growing either *Viburnum plicatum* 'Mariesii' which has distinctive tiers of white florets, or the mock orange (*Philadelphus*), which smells wonderful. The Mexican orange blossom (*Choisya ternata*) has another wonderful fragrance, this time on an evergreen bush which will flower in almost any position in the garden.

Mature town gardens often have a big shrub of the flowering currant (*Ribes sanguineum*), which has pink flowers, boring leaves and smells of cat pee. If you have one, dig it up and throw it away. *Ribes odoratum* makes a good replacement, with yellow flowers and a spicy scent, and *Ribes speciosum* has tiny fuchsia-like flowers of blood-red intensity and very spiky thorns. And what does one do about lilac? Lovely flower, shame about the plant. I think the answer is to let it grow for about three or four years and then, after flowering, cut it back almost to the ground – and do this every year thereafter. Give it a good soak after pruning and lay down a thick layer of compost as a mulch and it will produce quantities of big flowers next year without any of its horrible, sprawling growth. If you have acidic soil you are likely to grow rhododendrons, heathers and camellias, which is a pity, as nothing will induce me to like these plants. At the very least, consider the full range of alternatives first.

(RIGHT) A white lilac, *Syringa vulgaris*. The best flowers are produced on shrubs pruned hard after flowering.

TASKS FOR SPRING

- Buddlejas should be pruned hard in early spring, cutting them back to the lowest healthy pair of emerging leaves. Likewise dogwood (*Cornus sibirica*), which is grown for the winter colour of its stems; cut it back to the main stem or the ground as the leaves start to appear.

- The performance of all shrubs, whenever they flower, is improved with a light scattering of bonemeal and a thick mulch in mid-spring. Keep away any obvious weeds but otherwise that is the sum total of their care for the rest of the year.

(RIGHT) The hanging lines of *Stachyurus praecox* flowers are a sure sign that spring is starting to happen.

EARLY-SPRING FLOWERING SHRUBS

Chaenomeles (flowering quince)
Daphne mezereum
Forsythia
Magnolia stellata
Magnolia soulangiana
Mahonia aquifolium
Osmanthus (several)
Tree paeonies
Stachyurus praecox
Viburnum burkwoodii

MID-SPRING FLOWERING SHRUBS

Berberis
Genista lydia (broom)
Kerria japonica
Osmanthus burkwoodii
Ribes sanguineum
Viburnum opulus
Viburnum tomentosum

LATE-SPRING FLOWERING SHRUBS

Ceanothus
Choisya ternata
Daphne
Kolkwitzia
Philadelphus
Potentilla
Spiraea
Syringa (lilac)
Weigela

Summer shrubs

I KNOW THAT THE WHOLE SUBJECT OF ROSES CAN MYSTIFY AND TURN OFF A LOT OF PEOPLE. There are supposed complications about pruning and the flowers last only a few weeks, while the plants are ugly and spiky and it is all more trouble than it is worth. It is not. If you grow shrub roses (as opposed to hybrid Tea or Floribunda roses), they are no more trouble than any other shrub. They do not need any pruning, except to limit their size (depending on your garden), they have the most beautiful of all flowers on this planet, they smell fabulous and will flower long enough to justify their existence. On top of that, roses are the ideal host for clematis and make perfect companions for the larger herbs like lovage, fennel or rosemary. They are all very tough and do not need spraying or any special treatment at all. Most can easily be grown in a pot as long as you give them extra food every spring. There are masses of others just as suitable in their own way as those in the list on this page, but try one or some of them.

Just as in spring you want to integrate flowering shrubs with bulbs, so it is best to use summer-flowering shrubs as ingredients in the dish that is the garden rather than the meal itself. Because it works better with other plants, one shrub may often be more suitable than another shrub which has better flowers but spoils the overall mix. Again and again, when choosing plants, it is this compatibility that counts.

Shrubs with purple foliage can be a very useful foil at the back of a border. But in a small garden you want to be very sparing with it because it very easily sucks in light and dominates a border. Purple-leaved hazel is a very good colour and has the advantage that it can be cut hard (coppiced) down to the ground, which will both control its height and encourage rapid regrowth with bigger leaves.

Buddleja is ubiquitous but very often only grown because it is so easy. The paler-flowered forms can be very bland and not worth their space in a small garden, so go for the rich colours like 'Black Knight' or 'Royal Red' or a white form like 'White Cloud'. *Buddleja globosa* flowers before the more familiar *Buddleja davidii* and its flowers are orange balls.

If you have a very sunny, dry garden, cistus will do very well. These evergreen rock roses produce masses of flowers but each one lasts only a day. They are especially suitable if you have very poor soil or garden on chalk and they will even grow in the cracks between paving. *Cistus laurifolius* is the toughest of these Mediterranean plants and will tolerate anything our winters have to offer. They hate being moved once established.

There are too many sublime roses to choose one favourite, but the blood red *Rosa* 'Tuscany Superb' would be in anyone's top ten.

SUMMER ROSES

Rosa 'Blanc Double de Coubert'
R. x *centifolia* 'Chapeau de Napoléon'
Rosa 'Félicité Parmentier'
Rosa parvifolia (also 'Pompon de
Bourgogne')
Rosa 'Président de Sèze'
Rosa 'Tuscany Superb'

SUMMER-FLOWERING SHRUBS

Buddleja davidii
Cistus
Escallonia
Fuchsia
Hydrangea
Kalmia
Kolkwitzia
Lavandula
Potentilla
Roses

PURPLE-LEAVED SHRUBS

Berberis thunbergii
Corylus maxima 'Purpurea'
(purple-leaved hazel)
Cotinus coggygria 'Royal Purple'
(Smoke bush)
Sambucus nigra 'Guincho Purple'
Weigela florida 'Foliis Purpureis'

Autumn shrubs

SHRUBS DO THREE THINGS IN AUTUMN. A few flower, many change leaf colour in an attractive manner and some have decorative berries. The berries in particular belong to this season as rightly as blossom does to spring. Of course to get fruit you must leave the flower to develop and for many gardeners that goes against the puritanical grain of tidiness, as well as the more reasonable practice of cutting back faded flowerheads to stimulate the production of more. It is a trade-off between fewer, bedraggled flowers followed by berries or more flowers but no fruits of this particular season. Summer has plenty of flowers, but November needs all the colour it can get, so I plump for the berries every time.

The oddest of berries are those of **Callicarpa bodinieri giraldii,** which have a metallic sheen to their purple shanks. In my garden this shrub was very slow to establish, but it responds well to good soil and the berries last for ages. I like pyracantha's common name, 'firethorn', as it perfectly describes the way the berries blaze out from the unexceptional matt leaves. At a time of year when light and colour are at a premium, the firethorn more than earns its place in any garden. One should be as brash as possible with pyracantha, and **Pyracantha 'Orange Glow'** is as brash as they come.

Cotoneaster is slightly more subtle in its appeal and slightly less dramatic, but still jolly. There are far too many different cotoneasters to get to grips with unless you have a particular interest in them, and although most are completely unfussy about where you put them, as long as it is not boggy, it is common to use their adaptability for a very dry spot.

The **purple-leaved barberry (Berberis thunbergii atropurpurea)** is an excellent border plant in summer because of the depth and contrast that its purple leaves give to surrounding colours, but in autumn it is decorated with red berries which are rather more striking than the small yellow flowers that made them in spring. It is a really good example of choosing a plant that will work hard for you without you having to do any work for it.

Mahonia repens, Osmanthus decorus and **Daphne pontica** all have blue-black fruits that add depth to the slightly hysterical red of most berries. Plant them at the front of the border where they will not be lost in the shade. There will be autumn days when the whole garden seems to be cast adrift in a sodden grey haze. At such times berries come to the rescue, firing a flare of colour into the darkness. Make the most of these humble symbols of fruitfulness that will explode in a few months time.

No plant depends more for its place in the garden on its berries alone than *Callicarpa bodinieri* var. *giraldii* with its curiously metallic lilac fruit.

AUTUMN-FLOWERING SHRUBS

Fatsia japonica
Fuchsia
Genista tinctoria (broom)
Hydrangea
Mahonia x *media*
Vitex

SHRUBS WITH GOOD AUTUMN FOLIAGE

Amelanchier canadensis
Berberis
Callicarpa
Cleththra
Cornus alba (dogwood)
Corylopsis
Cotinus (smokebush)
Cotoneaster
Euonymus
Hamamelis (witch hazel)
Ribes odoratum
Rosa rugosa
Spiraea thunbergii
Rhus typhina (sumach)
Viburnum

SHRUBS WITH GOOD BERRIES

Berberis
Callicarpa
Chaenomeles (ornamental quince)
Cornus mas (dogwood)
Cotoneaster
Daphne mezereum
Euonymus
Pernettya
Pyracantha
Rosa rugosa
Sambucus
Skimmia japonica
Viburnum opulus

Winter shrubs

THERE IS A SMALL BAND OF SHRUBS THAT FLOWER IN WINTER, mostly on the bare branches so that their flowers are visible, odd and extremely welcome in the greyness of a northern winter. They have evolved to attract the attention of the few pollinating insects around in winter, free from the competition of hundreds of other, more showy plants. To aid this process most of them are strongly fragrant and make very good cut flowers, the woody stems lasting for days in water. Their weakness is a certain drabness in summer, which means that they must be planted at the back of a border where they can be masked or improved by something flowering in their resting season.

My favourite winter shrub is the **winter honeysuckle (*Lonicera fragrantissima*)** whose tiny white flowers are produced tentatively from before Christmas through to March. You may also find *L. standishii* and *L. x purpursii* sold as 'winter honeysuckle'. All three are very similar.

The **viburnums** are a useful, if unglamorous addition to the winter garden. When winter closes the show right down, then viburnums come into their modest own. The best known and certainly most ubiquitous of these is *Viburnum x bodnantense* 'Dawn', which has rose-pink bobbles of flower on its naked branches from late autumn through to spring. The florets are perfect little trumpets but they make a slightly irregular globe, as though shaped quickly by hand. 'Deben' is similar but with flowers that are almost white, just touched with a hint of pink that darkens as they age. Their upright growth makes a good support for something to clamber over and a clematis from the late-flowering Jackmanii group would be a perfectly suitable companion. Laurestinus (*Viburnum tinus*) is tolerant of sun or shade and almost any soil, but the flowers have no scent. *V.t.* 'Gwenllian' is sufficiently compact to justify its space in a small garden.

Mahonia **x *media*** has brilliant yellow, sweetly scented flowers and a spiky, distinctive shape. It is particularly useful for its ability to grow in shade. **Witch hazel (*Hamamelis mollis*)** has weird flowers, like sea anemones or scatters of shredded paper, ranging in colour from fire orange to egg-yolk yellow. A mature witch hazel is one of the best sights a January day can offer. In autumn the leaves colour beautifully. It can become rather large for a small garden, but if grown in a container or pruned regularly, it is not overpowering. **Winter-flowering jasmine (*Jasminum nudiflorum*)** is not showy but it never hurts the eye. It will grow and flower in complete shade and the buttery flowers are very pretty. Keep it cut back hard after flowering to stop it sprawling.

The witch hazel (*hamamelis x intermedia*) is typical of most winter shrubs in that its flowers are born on leafless stems.

The best winter shrub for scent is the winter-flowering honeysuckle, *Lonicera fragrantissima*, and a cut branch in a vase will fill a room with perfume.

WINTER-FLOWERING SHRUBS

Chimonanthus praecox (wintersweet)
Daphne mezereum
Garrya elliptica
Hamamelis (witch hazel)
Jasminum nudiflorum (winter jasmine)
Lonicera fragrantissima (winter-flowering honeysuckle)
Mahonia japonica
Mahonia x *media*
Viburnum x *bodnantense* 'Dawn'
Viburnum farreri
Viburnum tinus

Containers

How to get the best from containers

IF YOU HAVE ACCESS TO LIGHT AND AIR THEN YOU CAN STILL MAKE A COMPLETE GARDEN, even if it starts off as an area of deep concrete, punctuated by manhole covers and bounded by high walls. Almost anything will grow in a pot if there is sufficient room for the roots to grow and if it is adequately fed and watered. If you have a small backyard, your most pressing need will be for climbers and a generous-sized pot or tub will happily support a large climber; annual climbers also do very well in pots, supported by a wigwam of canes.

Growing plants in pots outside is simply another way of making a garden. Context is everything and you should plan and arrange your pots with the same care and attention to the overall scheme as you would if the plants were growing permanently into the ground. I like to think of pots as if they were pieces of furniture on wheels in a large room – you can move them around as necessary to make the most of both the furniture (the plants in the pots) and the room (the garden). This lack of permanence has a huge advantage. The pack of plants can be shuffled and rearranged according to your whim, according to the seasons, even to the different hours of the day as the sun moves round your yard, allowing for individual plant growth and the introduction of new subjects. Use this mobility to its full advantage and do not treat the pots as garden soil *manqué* but as

a quite different dimension of gardening. For one thing, the containers themselves are as much part of the decoration as the plants they contain. A cluster of smaller pots focused around a more permanently positioned large container always looks effective. On a practical level this means keeping the pots sufficiently small and light so that you can lift them when filled with plants in full foliar rig as well as with damp soil. For larger pots pulling them along on a sack 'trolley' will shift almost anything safely and easily.

Do not limit yourself to conventional clay pots. Enjoy the variety available to you – plants will grow in anything that has drainage holes and that will not collapse under the weight of wet soil. Old shopping baskets (lined with polythene), metal buckets, wooden boxes, shoes, tin cans, hats, chimney pots and saucepans all work as well as a conventional pot, at least in the short term.

Of course you can go the other way. You can pretend that you have a soil-based garden and build the ground upwards with a series of raised beds which, once made, are as fixed and unalterable as any ordinary garden border. The advantage over a 'natural' (gardening is never natural) border is that you can make up your perfect soil, preparing it to suit the plants you wish to grow. This is treating the whole yard like one vast container and is a perfectly reasonable, if labour-intensive, thing to do. However large these raised beds were, you would still have to treat them

Growing plants in pots means you can make groupings that would never work in a border, like the Mediterranean French lavender next to the moisture- and shade-loving *Hosta* behind it.

like pots and feed and water them extensively, as well as building in drainage so that the water could escape.

I think it much better to fill a small backyard with a miscellany of containers. It is the difference between a fitted kitchen bought from a catalogue and a room pieced together by intuition and chance until it *feels* right. I would go so far as to say that all good gardens, of any size or situation, are the better for having evolved by the latter method rather than being bought off the peg and assembled on site, however brilliant the designer.

PLANTING UP CONTAINERS

DO NOT TREAT YOUR POTS AS A HORTICULTURAL SIDE-SHOW OR A SECOND-BEST REPLACEMENT FOR A REAL GARDEN. Treating them seriously as your 'proper' garden initially means taking great care of your soil. To begin with, give each container an initial layer of stones or crocks (pieces of broken pot) as drainage. I always mix proprietary all-purpose coir- or soil-based (avoid peat) compost with perlite at a ratio of about one part perlite to three parts compost. Vermiculite is almost as good and horticultural grit is very useful but perlite seems to be able to simultaneously help drainage and retain moisture, as well as keeping the soil open so that plant roots run freely. It is very good stuff. When you are planting, make it a rule always to put in at least 2.5cm (1in) of drainage material at the bottom as well as leaving at least 2.5cm (1in) between the surface of the soil and the rim of the container. Stick to this even in the smallest pots. The space at the top is for watering, otherwise water just bounces off before it has a chance to soak in.

An insulating layer on the inside of terracotta pots will reduce evaporation in summer and frost and wind-chill damage to roots in winter. This is especially important with evergreens in an exposed position. Thin polystyrene works well or insulating foam can be sprayed into the pot, smeared round and then cut cleanly after it dries. This will also make the pot lighter and easier to move. Using polystyrene chips instead of stones or crocks is another way to lighten the pot.

(LEFT) One of the great advantages of growing hostas in a pot is that they are less likely to be attacked by slugs and snails and much easier to protect with a layer of vaseline around the outside of the pot.

(RIGHT) Balconies are the perfect opportunity to transform a building with plants.

WATERING CONTAINERS

YOUR CONTAINERS ARE GOING TO NEED LOTS OF WATER. A plant in a pot requires a greater volume of water than its garden-planted counterpart and a large, fast-growing one much more. I water our pots until the water going in at the top seems to be coming out equally fast at the bottom. If this happens too quickly it means either that the drainage is too free or, more likely, that the plant is rootbound and dried up and there is not enough soil in the container to absorb any water. In this case, submerge the whole thing, pot and all, in a bucket of water until the bubbles stop rising. This may take a good half hour if it is very dry. Repot the plant into a bigger container so there is enough soil for the roots to grow into.

There are two schools of thought about installing an irrigation system for pots. One says that in a small yard or roof garden it is cheap, easy and prevents any risk of drought damage and it is therefore crazy not to do it. The other points out that watering is the main horticultural activity of such a garden and by watering the pots daily you get a chance to check each plant and to simply look at them in a focused fashion. I think that roof gardens generally need an irrigation system because their plants are so prone to water-loss through evaporation, but that the watering-as-contemplation school has much to commend it. A series of drip feeds coming off a ring pipe is best for pots, dripping water gently down to the roots rather than spraying the leaves.

If you overwater or if you have poor drainage, you are going to invite fungal problems like powdery mildew which will manifest itself as grey powder on the leaves. Raise pots on crocks so the roots do not sit in water, keep water to the soil, not the plant leaves, and ensure plenty of ventilation around them.

One way of reducing moisture loss is to clump small pots together. This cuts down evaporation and creates a little microclimate of moisture, trapping and using evaporation as it occurs. If you go away for more than a day or two, place the containers in saucers or trays filled with water and move the pots into the shade.

FEEDING PLANTS IN POTS

As a rule, bought compost has only enough goodness for the first couple of months. You will have to feed regularly after that, especially for fast-growing plants; plant food is available in different forms, with balanced ratios of minerals. The two main needs are nitrogen for green growth and potash for strong roots (which immediately produces healthy flowers and fruits). Go steady on the nitrogen as a sudden spurt of top growth as a result of overfeeding often makes plants prone to disease or pests and will not be balanced by equal root growth. **Bonemeal** is beneficial if a small handful is added when planting and each subsequent spring. **Liquid seaweed** added to the watering can every week or fortnight is good for trees and shrubs: it helps develop woody growth and works very well as a monthly foliar feed, sprayed directly onto the leaves. Proprietary **tomato fertiliser** is high in potash so it helps any fruiting or flowering plant.

Never re-use old compost. It may still look serviceable but most of the goodness will be gone from it. It is best recycled via the compost heap (and you can get very good enclosed compost makers, so there is no excuse). Prune plant growth so there is less demand on the roots and give a mulch of compost and bonemeal every autumn and winter. Mulch leafy plants like hostas with grit to deter snails, which will strip their juicy foliage overnight.

(LEFT) Grasses grow well in pots and look terrific. Here *Festuca eskia* grows next to the felt-leaved lavendar, *Lavandula lanata*.

(RIGHT) A bucket makes a good pot but must have drainage holes, especially for a Mediterranean plant like this thyme.

Window boxes

TO BEGIN, A STERN WARNING ABOUT WINDOW BOXES: always consider the effect as a whole rather than any particular plant in it. One dying leaf or unsuccessful flower will ruin an entire window box. Five out of six plants in the group may be perfect, but if the sixth is not right the whole box looks terrible. The secret is to keep things simple. So many window boxes are crammed with a medley of unrelated plants – any one of which looks fine on its own, but as an isolated group against the side of a building they become an unharmonious mess. There is a tendency to confuse simplicity with dullness but the exact opposite is true in gardening. Simplicity is very hard to achieve in gardens and window boxes are one of the few chances to get it perfectly right. My favourite place for window boxes is Venice, where almost every building overlooking a tiny canal will have a window box beneath each green-shuttered window and every one will be overflowing with the same plant – ivy-leaf geranium. The effect is stunning.

Any trailing plant can look effective in a window box, whereas few upright ones appear comfortable. An exception to this rule are bulbs, which always look great. But obey the law of simplicity and do not mix them. Use just daffodils or just tulips and make sure they are all identical. This can be made more sophisticated by having a succession of flowers, with new growth pushing past the previous growth as it fades. Plant bulbs in layers, with the biggest and latest to flower at the bottom. I would suggest daffodils, grape hyacinths and snowdrops in three layers. Pack them in as tightly as they will fit and keep them watered as they grow. You will have to dig the bulbs up and repot them all after the daffodils have finished flowering, if you do not want a mess of yellowing leaves throughout May and June.

I think it a great mistake to plant any small trees or even shrubs in a window box unless they are strictly formal and repetitive. You can just get away with clipped box but I hardly see the point. Stick to plants that spill out, giving the window box a sense of overflowing with plant life. You must of course choose the plants that you like for a window box but, as a guide, my favourites for this role are listed opposite.

Many window boxes are sold without drainage holes. These are essential, so drill plenty of large holes in the bottom and cover them with at least 2.5cm (1in) of gravel or stones big enough not to fall through the holes. Fill with potting compost and perlite as for containers (see page 116). Do not overfill the box but leave 2.5cm (1in) clear at the top to allow room for water. A full, wet window box can be very heavy, so make sure that it is securely fixed to the wall.

FAVOURITE WINDOW-BOX PLANTS

Alchemilla mollis
Argyranthemum (marguerites)
Artemisia
Ferns
Galanthus nivalis (snowdrops)
Hedera (ivy)
Hosta
Muscari (grape hyacinths)
Narcissus (daffodils)
Nicotiana (tobacco plants)
Osteospermum
Pelargonium peltatum (ivy-leaf
   geranium)
Sedum
Tropaeolum (nasturtiums)
Tulipa

Two contrasting approaches to window boxes: (LEFT) A bright splash of colour with *Pelargoniums*, *Lobelia* and paint and (RIGHT) a more naturalistic mix of grasses and *Osteospermum*.

Fast food

Why grow food?

I MUST CONFESS A BIAS HERE – little in gardening gives me so much pleasure or makes so much sense as growing something delicious to eat just outside my back door. If it can also look beautiful, then the gardening circle is made complete. The truth is that many vegetables, herbs and fruits are no harder to grow than anything else in the garden and they need not take up very much space. Much can be grown in containers and many leaf vegetables and herbs fit perfectly well into a flower border. However, most food crops like sun and will produce a much richer harvest if grown with the protection of a south- or west-facing wall.

We live in an age where we have never been so divorced from our source of food. We are seduced – for all the obvious and good reasons – by fast food and by marketing that tells us food is organic or fresh, even though we have no way of knowing exactly what that means. The freshest and fastest food in the world is in your garden. You can go outside and select a lettuce and a handful of herbs and prepare them for the table in five minutes. No meal could be easier, fresher or more quickly put together. The added bonus is that if you choose your varieties with any care at all, your home-grown fruit, herbs and vegetables are going to be tastier than anything you can buy. If you have a garden and you like food, then it is mad not to grow your own.

(ABOVE) Taking the table to the food in a fabulous back garden, growing vegetables, fruit and herbs.

(LEFT) Pears grown as a cordon against a brick wall, taking up little space but producing lots of fruit.

Having become excited by the idea, you must be realistic about the limitations of your small back garden. You are not growing food for any right-on reason; this is pure hedonism and, unless you want to turn the entire garden into a vegetable patch (which is not a bad idea at all), you will only have room for a few favourite and suitable items. These will have to be especially useful in the kitchen, especially quick growing, especially toothsome or especially decorative. I would suggest that a careful selection of herbs, some salad crops such as lettuce, endive and rocket and one or two fruit trees could be fitted into a tiny space or into containers.

I shall expand on the subject of herbs and salad crops over the next few pages, but first a brief word about fruit trees. If you have a south- or west-facing wall, this makes an ideal place to train an espaliered (ornamentally trained) fruit tree. Resist any temptation to grow a familiar apple like Cox's Orange Pippin; they are notoriously difficult to grow and you can buy perfectly good fruit. Instead grow a really delicious pear like Doyenne du Comice so that you can savour a few truly ripe pears a year – which money cannot buy. Or grow figs, apricots or peaches, all of which ripen well on a warm wall.

Herbs

HERBS HAVE BEEN GROWN at the heart of every garden since plants were first cultivated. A town garden entirely based upon herbs would be a beautiful, calming and practical place and not the least bit limited. Fortunately most herbs grow easily, and all the Mediterranean herbs, such as rosemary, thyme, marjoram, fennel and sage, are actually happiest on a poorly nourished, well-drained, light soil – a description that exactly fitted my own London garden. But even if your garden is shaded and the soil heavy, you can still grow a wide variety of herbs. Parsley, angelica, comfrey, caraway, chervil, chives, fennel, horseradish, all mints, sorrel, sweet cicely, bergamot and lemon balm, all tolerate or even prefer moist conditions.

The herbs that you use regularly in cooking need to be as close to the kitchen door as possible. But I like the idea of having a small, essential selection like parsley, mint, sage, chives and rosemary right by the back door and then a much wider range at the very end of the garden. Having parts of the garden that you have to journey to – even if that is only a few paces – makes the space feel larger and is more fun than pure function. In the winter the remote herb garden can shut up shop and be visited only weekly while one reaches out of the back door for a handful of rosemary rather more often.

(ABOVE) Curly parsley makes a good edible edging to a border.

(LEFT) Mint growing with *Myosotis* and fennel. Mint can be very invasive, so unless you are happy to let it spread indiscriminately, plant it within an old bucket or pot with a hole in its bottom for drainage.

SOWING HERBS

All herbs are easy to grow from seed and for the price of one plant you can practically stock an entire street with a year's worth of herbs. Sow the seeds as thinly as possible in seed trays or pots. As soon as the seedlings have two 'true' leaves rather than the initial 'seed leaves', lift them carefully and transplant at wider spacing or into individual pots. A week before they are large enough to plant out (common sense will tell you when this is) put them outside during the day to 'harden off', or become acclimatised to outdoor temperatures. Water them well after planting. In my experience rosemary, chives, thyme, marjoram, basil, dill, lovage and fennel are all particularly easy to grow from seed.

Herbs

WHICH HERBS TO GROW?

Mint grows very easily but only two types are really useful in the kitchen: spearmint (*Mentha spicata*) and applemint (*Mentha rotundifolia*). Peppermint (*Mentha piperata*) is used for making mint tea. Once established, mint will take over an entire border. Sink an old bucket or plastic pot with the bottom knocked out into the ground and fill it with soil. Plant your mint in this to stop it spreading – or grow it in a container.

Three herbs that are grown primarily for their structural value prefer a dry, sunny, position. **Fennel** (*Foeniculum vulgare*) comes in two shades, green and bronze; the leaves make a wonderful aniseedy addition to a grilled trout and their tall but delicate outline is something that I would not be without in any mixed border. **Lovage** (*Levisticum officinale*) grows to over 1m (3ft) high and has a hollow stalk with fleshy green leaves; it can be eaten like celery and the leaves added to salads and stews. **Dill** (*Anethum graveolens*) is another tall umbellifer (from the cow-parsley family) but likes poor, well-drained soil; sow or plant every few months for a succession of plants and keep them well-watered, otherwise they quickly go to seed.

Marjoram is indispensable and very easy to grow as long as the drainage is good and it gets some sunshine. I get confused between oregano and marjoram but, for the record, *Origanum vulgare* is known in Britain as wild marjoram and in the Mediterranean as oregano. *Origanum onites* is pot marjoram and *Origanum majorana* is sweet marjoram, which has perhaps the best flavour.

Rosemary loves heat and dry soil and is one of the few plants that can be left unwatered throughout the summer. For a small garden *Rosmarinus officinalis* 'Miss Jessop' is ideal because it makes a tall, upright bush as opposed to the rather lax, sprawling habit of most rosemary (which can, of course, be its charm in a larger garden).

Parsley (*Petroselinum crispum*) likes a good rich soil with plenty of water and will grow happily in partial shade. Flat-leaved parsley (*Petroselinum crispum* 'French') is much the best for culinary purposes and rather hardier than the curly-leaved variety that appears so ubiquitously as a ridiculous 'garnish'. Parsley seed can be slow to germinate. Sow in a row directly in the ground in April, spacing the seeds thinly. Thin to 8cm (3in) as the seedlings appear (be ruthless about this – the plants become quite large and need the space). Make another sowing in August for harvesting the following April and May. The key to parsley is water – never let the soil dry out or else it will 'bolt' and develop flowerheads rather than leaves. Parsley is biennial so will not last into a second season.

Where you can grow parsley you can also grow **chives** as both flourish in rich, slightly shaded conditions. Chives are much easier than parsley, however, lasting for years. The flowerheads are edible, beautiful in the garden and on the plate, but the plant will last longer if kept regularly cropped back. Over-large, mature plants can be divided with a spade and replanted to make a number of new ones.

Basil (*Ocimum basilicum*) is my favourite herb. It is easy to grow but needs lots of sunshine, rich soil and plenty of water to do well. It will not survive even the tiniest touch of frost, so it can only be grown in the summer months in Britain. Either sow seeds on a windowsill in April to plant out in the middle of May or buy plants ready to plant out. Pinch out the tops as they grow and harvest the leaves from each plant to encourage fresh growth.

Common sage (*Salvia officinalis*) is a tough perennial that benefits from a good cutting back each spring. Purple sage looks good in a border with its bronze leaves and white sage has white flowers as opposed to the pinky/purple ones of common sage. Sage is one of the easiest garden plants to take from cuttings.

HERBS IN CONTAINERS

Herbs are very easy to grow in a container or window box. Make sure that you have extra drainage in the base and mix the potting compost with vermiculite or horticultural grit. A survival kit might consist of:

Rosemary (*Rosmarinus officinalis* 'Miss Jessop' – upright and space-saving)

Sage (*Salvia officinalis* 'Albiflora', narrow-leaved)

Parsley (flat-leaved *Petroselinum crispum* 'French')

Applemint (*Mentha rotundifolia*) and spearmint (*M. spicata*)

Lemon thyme (*Thymus* x *citriodorus*)

Basil (*Ocimum basilicum*) and perhaps purple basil

Sweet marjoram (*Origanum majorana*)

Chives (*Allium schoenoprasum*)

HERBS FOR MOIST SHADE

Parsley (*Petroselinum crispum*) Make two sowings: in April and August

Angelica (*Angelica archangelica*) Biennial; grows to 2m (6ft)

Lovage (*Levisticum officinale*) Perennial, lasting several years

Chervil (*Anthriscus cerefolium*) Annual; must be used fresh

Chives (*Allium schoenoprasum*) Hardy perennial

Lemon balm (*Melissa officinalis*) Hardy perennial (rather invasive)

Mint (*Mentha* species) All mints are rampant, so restrain!

Bergamot (*Monarda didyma*) Wonderful flowers

Purple basil looks great and tastes good
(but perhaps not as good as green basil).

HERBS FOR DRY, SUNNY CONDITIONS

Thyme (*Thymus vulgaris*) Wonderful scent

Marjoram (*Oregano majorana*) Although perennial, treat as an annual

Rosemary (*Rosmarinus officinalis*) Woody shrub: *hates* cold damp

Basil (*Ocimum basilicum*) Tender annual killed by first frost

Sage (*Salvia officinalis*) Cut back each spring

Dill (*Anethum graveolens*) Needs watering frequently

Fennel (*Foeniculum vulgare*) Perennial: comes in bronze or green

Bay (*Laurus nobilis*) A tree that needs protection from frost

Tarragon (*Artemisia dracunculus*) Perennial with yellow flowers

Salad crops

THERE IS NOT THE SPACE HERE OR IN YOUR GARDEN for a full range of vegetables, but any garden, be it a tiny patch of yard, has room for a few salad crops, a group in which I include lettuces, rocket, endive, chicory, radicchio and spinach.

LETTUCES

The skill in growing lettuce lies in successional crops, the organisation of a constant supply from your limited resources. A packet of lettuce seed will produce, in ideal circumstances, a hundred lettuce, all ready to eat at the same time. The normal process of thinning cuts that number by three-quarters, but most small households do not need more than two lettuces a day. If you grow three or four kinds, it follows that three a week of each variety is ample. Therefore the secret is to sow a quarter of a packet at a time, at 10-day intervals, so that each crop follows the other like waves on a shore.

It is important to know how long the process from sowing to consumption will take, and in the table below I give the time it would normally take for a lettuce to fully mature. This can be reduced by as much as three weeks by eating the thinnings and deliberately harvesting immature plants that will taste better.

Most lettuce are best sown in lines, or drills, marked by your finger, and about 15cm (6in) apart. Sow them about 1cm (½ in) deep and as thinly as possible. It is not a bad idea to water the drill before you sow the seed, so that the seeds lie on wet ground. Make sure your hands are absolutely dry and, holding the seed in the palm of one hand, squeeze a pinch of seed at a time between the thumb and forefinger of the other hand.

Lettuce needs cool temperatures to germinate, and may become dormant if the soil is above 20°C (68°F). This means that you can make sowings from mid-March to July and then again in August as the nights cool, through to October. The October sowing will not be ready for harvesting until April/May of the following year. Lettuces vary in size, but I would say that no type of lettuce needs to be more than 15cm (6in) apart from its neighbour. It is far better to have two small plants than one whopper. Cos varieties tend to perform best under this regime, particularly 'Little Gem', 'Lobjoit's Green', 'Valmaine' and 'Winter Density' (for early or late sowing). 'Tom Thumb' is a butterhead that, as its name implies, forms a compact lettuce which tastes delicious.

This sowing technique applies to all lettuces, but 'cut-and-come again' or loose-leaf lettuce varieties have a different method of harvesting. The leaves are simply picked just as you might pick herbs; you are in effect pruning the lettuce and it will respond by producing more growth. This process will normally provide two and sometimes as many as four crops before the plant is exhausted.

OTHER SALAD CROPS

Radicchio, chicory and **endive** are closely related, although most chicory needs blanching to get rid of its bitterness. Endive can be made sweeter by tying the leaves together at the top, but I like the slight bitterness of moss-curled endive when mixed with a sweet lettuce like 'Lobjoit's Green' cos. Radicchio is slow to develop and is best sown in mid-May for harvesting from September.

You can buy a packet of mixed salad seeds called either **'Saladini'** or **'Saladesi'** which will include cos lettuce, red and green 'cutting' lettuce, salad rocket, sugarloaf chicory, curly endive and corn salad. They do best sown in early spring or late summer and tend to grow fast, especially in May and September. You can harvest the seedlings as they grow, cutting them with scissors, plucking leaves with your hands or pulling them to thin and make room for bigger plants as they mature. This is a really good way to grow a dish rather than just ingredients. **Rocket** is very easy to grow, but only in spring and autumnal coolness. It needs a lot of water in summer to stop it bolting almost overnight. It is best to make a sowing in March, then another in mid-August which will last through to March and April. Sow it just like lettuce, cutting entire plants to the ground with a knife as and when needed, encouraging it to grow fresh young leaves rather than letting them develop into mature plants. **Spinach** is one of the easiest spring crops and the young leaves make the best spring salad. Spinach needs a lot of water and some shade if it is not to bolt and go to seed, so is best sown in March and April, then again in August.

LEAF CROPS

NAME	TYPE	SIZE	MATURATION	NOTES
'Tom Thumb'	Early crisphead	Small	65 days	Slow to bolt; old variety
'Little Gem'	Cos	Small	80 days	Delicious; 1 lettuce per person
'Valdor'	Butterhead	Medium		Sow autumn for early spring harvest
'Salad Bowl'	Loose-leaf	Large	80 days	Leaves picked throughout summer
'Red Salad Bowl'	Loose-leaf	Large	80 days	Red leaves regrow when picked
'Lollo Rossa'	Loose-leaf	Medium	80 days	Leaves frilled with red
'Lobjoit's Green'	Cos	Large	80 days	Upright, crisp, delicious
'Green Curled'	Endive	Medium	80 days	Slightly bitter leaves, good in salad
'Sugar Loaf'	Chicory	Medium	90 days	Sow late summer for winter eating; needs no blanching
'Witloof'	Chicory	Small	150 days	Chicory for blanching and making 'chicons'
'Alouette'	Radicchio	Small	150 days	Essential growing! Sow May to August for autumn/winter
'Lamb's Lettuce'		Small	Winter	Excellent winter crop
Celtuce		Medium	75 days	Celery-flavoured lettuce
'Sigmaleaf'	Spinach	Medium	50 days	Pick young leaves as they appear for salads; needs water
Winter purslane	Miner's lettuce	Small	Winter	Very good winter crop; needs shade
Flat-leaf parsley	Parsley	Small	75 days	Grow for salads; water well
Rocket		Small	75 days	Very distinctive taste; pick when young

Avoiding trouble

Pests and diseases

IT ALWAYS AMAZES ME HOW WORKED UP PEOPLE GET ABOUT THE THINGS THAT CAN GO WRONG IN A GARDEN. At any one moment in every single garden there are thousands of insects and animals, scores of weeds and dozens of diseases all happily getting on with their place in the scheme of things. That's the way it is. The only means of stopping it is by artificially interrupting the cycle with chemicals. That is stupid, because it halts the natural system of checks and balances that will inevitably evolve in a garden, and incredibly short-sighted because while it might improve the quality of a few blooms this year, it is polluting the environment irreversibly. We can often see very specific results initially, but the side-effects and knock-on effects may take years to work through. Chemical measures are also expensive, time-consuming and extremely naff. Don't do it.

It must be understood that gardens are not natural places. You are trying to cram into a little space a range of plants and of different growing conditions that would very rarely evolve in the wild. In doing so you are increasing the chances of disease and pest infestation. That is a fact of gardening life. Some of these pests and diseases can be pretty devastating in the short term, so over the next few pages I shall point out some ways of dealing with them. But the real solution is to have a healthy garden. Use lots of organic compost in the soil, do not be too tidy so that you make sure you have plenty of cover for birds and insects that will feed on would-be pests, collect all leaves and compost them and accept the limitations and implications of the climate and soil. If the plants are happy in your garden (not in a talk-to-the-flowers kind of way, but insofar as they are growing in an environment that they like) and are healthy, then they will resist most attacks by pest or disease. If you force them to behave unnaturally they will be much more prone to trouble. As with almost everything in the garden, it comes down to common sense.

SEAWEED SOLUTION

This is the single most valuable aid the gardener has, and the only one that I use at all. Use it as a weak spray to promote strong, healthy plants and to help actively against aphids, brown rot in fruit, damping-off in seedlings and tomatoes and leaf-curl virus. It is better to apply a weak solution every week or so than to give a big hit every couple of months.

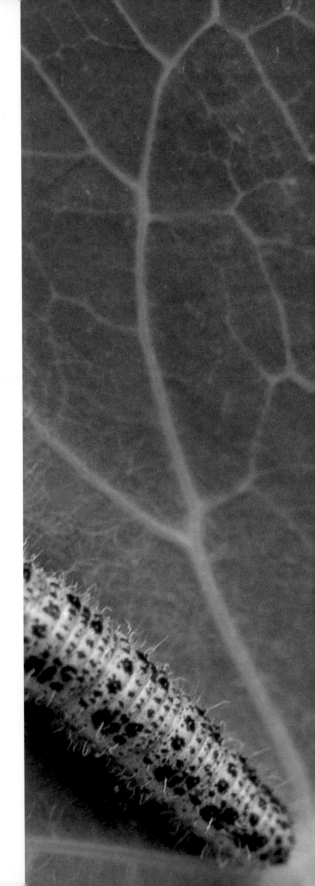

Pests

ANY GARDEN IS RICH IN PLANT FOOD AND WILL ATTRACT PESTS LIKE GREENFLY, CATERPILLARS, THRIPS, SLUGS AND SNAILS OR EARWIGS. This is inevitable. Traditional horticultural thinking was that anything that ate 'your' plants uninvited was a pest and should be destroyed. Thankfully we are all now more enlightened and realise that a surfeit of one kind of animal will result in a rise in its natural predator, followed by a natural decline in the prey and a subsequent fall in the numbers of the predator. And so it continues. Trouble occurs only when there is a shortage of predators.

In town gardens the worst pests are likely to be slugs and snails. Snails live in the loose brickwork that is inevitable in old town gardens and slugs live in the soil. Both do their pillaging mainly after dark. Try going out into the garden the next warm, damp evening and shine a torch around. The chances are that the garden will be slowly writhing with slimy bodies. In an experiment 27,500 slugs were taken from one small garden without making any noticeable difference to slug activity. Densities of 200 slugs per square metre are moderate.

Slug pellets are the usual method of control, and to a certain extent they work. The chemical in them is metaldehyde, which is noxious to humans as well as slugs. The pellets look rather like sweeties and are therefore a bit dodgy if you have small children, as well as looking ugly in themselves; it is reckoned that even intensive use of slug pellets will only rid your garden of 10 per cent of its slug population. The best method of control is to go out with a torch and a bucket and physically pick them up. Put salty water in the bucket, which will kill them, and throw them away the next day.

Beetles eat slugs, but the trouble is that for their predations to be effective you have to create a beetle-friendly garden, and using slug pellets and chemical solutions will harm the beetles as well as the slugs. Beetles like cover, so leave dead wood and leaves around for them. Hedgehogs eat beetles but they prefer a juicy slug. They are to be encouraged into the garden but, once again, this means no slug pellets. Toads eat young slugs and thrushes eat snails. The law of supply and demand says that in order to get these attractive additions to the garden there has to be a supply of food – so no snails, no thrushes. No slugs – no hedgehogs, toads or beetles.

The best way to deal with slugs or snails in the short term is to physically get between them and the object of their hunger. Any form of barrier will do, although gravel or grit is probably the most effective. Spread this as a mulch around hostas, delphiniums and all other susceptible plants and the slugs and snails will avoid crawling over the abrasive surface. Slugs eat rotting vegetation, so if you are digging compost or manure into the soil, you will improve things by making sure it is very well decayed before putting it into the ground, thereby providing less for the slugs to eat. Encourage as many birds as possible into the garden by planting trees, shrubs and bushy climbers. Leave on all seedheads until spring and do not be too tidy in the garden lest you tidy away insects, larvae and other bird-food.

COMPANION PLANTING

There is not room here to go into all the theory of companion planting, but some plants can protect their neighbours from pests. **Garlic** is particularly effective at protecting roses from greenfly, blackspot and mildew. **Chives** will also discourage aphids. **Marigolds** attract predators such as hoverflies, which will eat greenfly, as do **poached-egg plants** (*Limnanthes douglasii*).

PEST	DAMAGE	ACTION
Aphids	Feed on plant sap	Encourage ladybirds and hoverflies or spray with soft soap (a solution of washing-up liquid).
Blackfly	Particularly bad on broad beans, dahlias, nasturtiums and poppies	As for aphids.
Carrot fly	Larvae eat carrots, parsnips and celery	Sow thinly and erect a low screen around carrots. Avoid thinning during the day.
Earwigs	Eat dahlias and chrysanthemums	Trap them in jam jars.
Greenfly	Spoil roses	Plant garlic around roses, spray with a solution of soft soap, derris or Pyrethrum (natural insecticides). Wash with clear water soon after.
Millipedes	Eat bulbs and many plant roots	Dig thoroughly, improve drainage.
Scale insects	Lives on fruit trees and bushes	Paint with white spirit.
Slugs and snails	Eat all soft and decaying leaves	Use sharp mulches such as grit.
Thrips (thunderflies)	Live on sap	Spray with Pyrethrum or derris.

Disease

THE HEALTHY GARDEN HAS ITS OWN
INTERNAL MICRO-BALANCE THAT IS ALSO
IN EQUILIBRIUM WITH THE LARGER LOCAL
ENVIRONMENT WHICH – we rather forlornly hope – is
in synch. with the ecosystem at large. We know that mankind has
been busily doing its best to foul up the planet for the past 50
years but the garden is one place where you can control things
and change that. It is up to you. To my mind it is clear: only an
ignorant fool tries to make a garden that is out of tune with the
natural balance of things. But it is useful to be able to recognise
problems when they occur and to know what reasonable action
to take.

Most disease in gardens is fungal, resulting from over-feeding,
over-crowding and over-watering. To a certain extent all three
conditions are endemic in a garden of any kind. We deliberately
cram plants in a small space, feed them with extra goodness and
water them as much as regulations and time will allow. To stop
any of these going too far, some of the time, is impossible.

Good drainage is always important in the prevention of
disease. As a rule this implies making the soil more free-draining
by adding organic matter, digging deeply, adding grit or sand or
even laying drains if the ground is very wet. Occasionally, for
example on sandy soils, it means improving the soil's moisture-
retention to stop nutrients leaching out too fast – and adding
organic material is the best way to do this.

Try and prevent any trauma in the life of a plant which would
increase its chance of disease. The most obvious example would
be failing to water a plant in a container, causing it to suffer stress,
but disease could equally be a result of over-watering, planting
out when the soil is too cold or not protecting a delicate plant
from frost or from cold wind. It all comes down to sensible, un-
neurotic care for the plants as they grow. The table gives the
most common diseases you are likely to come across and the best
way of preventing and dealing with them.

DISEASE	INDICATION	ACTION
Botrytis	Grey mould fungus on leaves and stems	**Increase airflow and reduce watering.**
Canker	Dead, wrinkled stems and bark	**Prune carefully, removing diseased branches on trees, especially fruit.**
Coral spot	An orange or pink fungus that grows on the wood of trees and shrubs	**Prune back to healthy wood.**
Damping off	A fungus that kills seedlings	**Sow thinly, do not over-water and provide plenty of ventilation.**
Mildew	Makes white or yellow powder	**Caused by dry roots. Water well and mulch to retain moisture.**
Rust	Orange patches on leaves (especially roses)	**Often a sign of too much nitrogen. Spray with seaweed solution on leaves and stems.**
Leaf curl	Leaves curl up and drop off	**Spray with seaweed solution as leaves open; burn diseased leaves.**
Honey fungus	Toadstools at stems or base of trunk of trees	**Disaster! Remove every trace of plant and burn.**

(FAR LEFT) Lupins are prone to attack by lupin aphid, feeding off the sap and covering the leaves with honeydew and sooty mould, causing the plant to wilt.

(LEFT) Rust, as on these *Hypericum* leaves, is a fungal infection on leaves caused mainly by damp, warm, stagnant conditions.

Dealing with weeds

IT IS A WELL-REHEARSED AXIOM THAT A WEED IS MERELY A PLANT IN THE WRONG PLACE, and I often find tomatoes growing by the hundred in borders where they have seeded themselves via the compost heap. But on the whole we all know what weeds are, although differentiating a weed from a seedling, particularly in spring, can be confusing.

There are two kinds of weed, annual and perennial. **Annual weeds** grow from seed and survive only one growing season. A thick crop of annual weeds present no problem and can even be seen as a good sign, as they indicate that the soil is fertile. They are easy to pull up and can be added to the compost heap. It is very common for a mulch of rotted manure to be followed by a rash of weeds, the seeds of which have been sitting in the manure waiting to germinate. The annual weeds you are likely to encounter in your garden are groundsel, chickweed, fat-hen and annual meadow grass.

Perennial weeds survive for more than two growing seasons – sometimes for many years. Dock seeds can apparently lie dormant in the soil for up to 90 years, waiting for the soil to be disturbed before germinating. I like the thought that all over the country there are docks emerging from a century-old sleep, conceived in an age before cars, Hitler, television and Häagen-Dazs ice cream. We should be slapping preservation orders on them, not destroying them. Other common perennial weeds are nettle, bindweed, ground elder, couch grass and thistle. Where annual weeds are merely a nuisance, perennial weeds are a real problem.

DEALING WITH ANNUAL WEEDS

There is a saying: 'One year's seeding is seven years' weeding', meaning that it takes seven years for all the seeds of one crop to die out in the soil. As a single big plant of fat-hen (*Chenopodium album*) can produce 70,000 seeds, we are talking a lot of weeds. A weedy area of ground may contain as many as 15,000 weed seeds per square metre. So it is vital to destroy annual weeds before they set seed. Weeds have the same nutritional and cultivation requirements as the plants that we do want, and compete hungrily with them for available food and moisture. By removing annual weeds we are effectively feeding and watering the plants that remain.

The best way to deal with annuals is by a two-pronged attack of mulching, which keeps the ground dark so most seeds cannot germinate, and hoeing. I once asked a craggy old boy with an amazingly lush, productive garden what his secret was, probing for country magic; he pulled me close and whispered hoarsely, 'I never lets that hoe rest'. Another old gardener once told me fiercely that if you can ever see a weed then it is a sure sign that you are not hoeing enough. The point is clear: always keep on top of the weeds while they are small. Best for annual weeds is the Dutch hoe which you push through the soil just below the surface, cutting the weeds off from their roots. The sharper you keep it, the easier it is to work and the more effective the results. Hoe when the ground is dry, preferably in the morning, and the weeds will die in the sun. If the weeds are big, collect them up and put them on the compost heap.

ERADICATING PERENNIAL WEEDS

There is only one foolproof method of dealing with perennial weeds: remove the plant before it seeds and dig every last scrap of root from the ground, then burn the lot. But there are weeds like horsetail, horseradish and Japanese knotweed with roots of enormous depth and resilience. Horsetail can go down 2.5m (8ft) and knotweed can be as tough as steel hawsers. Certain other weeds, like ground elder, bindweed and couch grass, have a habit of winding in among the roots of plants you wish to keep so they have a safe haven from the most diligent of weeding.

There is no easy answer and no let-up in the battle. However, taking the following steps will help you to keep on top of the problem.

1. Dig where you can. Be meticulous: it is better to clear a square metre (sq yd) properly than to do 10 sq m roughly. Couch, bindweed and ground elder will grow into rampant plants from a piece of root the size of a half-used match.

2. Use weedkillers. Only a simpleton is politically correct about the use of chemical measures against weeds. But use only glyphosate (Roundup, Tumbleweed) which becomes harmless on contact with soil and kills only green tissue. Treat weedkillers with great care and use them strictly according to the instructions on the packaging; if used responsibly they are safe. Glyphosate sprays are particularly effective on couch grass, docks, thistles, bindweed and ground elder, but less good on nettles, horseradish or horsetail.

3. Cut and cut again. If you have a border that is infested with any of the weeds that resist glyphosate sprays, and which you do not have the time or inclination to dig clean, regular hoeing with a sharp hoe that slices the plant off just below the surface will dramatically weaken the weed's growth. Or you can take a longer-term view: lift the plants you wish to keep (washing the roots clean under a tap to clean out any trace of weed roots tangled among them) and sow the border with rye grass. This should be mown weekly for at least a year. The mowing will weaken the weeds considerably, while strengthening the grass,

Nettles are a weed and sting horribly but they do attract butterflies, aphid-eating wasps and make good soup.

which in turn will suppress the weeds. After a couple of years the plot can be sprayed off to kill the grass and converted back to a border.

4. Mulch with black plastic. This looks horrible and takes at least two years to be effective, so it should be a last resort, but it does work. Cover the plastic with a mulch of gravel or bark to make it look less hideous.

Finally, weeding is something that must be done little and often. Never let that hoe rest.

Accessories

Inside out

A GARDEN IS THE SUM OF *ALL* ITS PARTS, including those that the eye conveniently slides past or excuses as temporary. So, tables, chairs, the washing on the line, the tools that you use and the hosepipe snaking up the garden path, all *are* the garden and should be given as careful consideration on account of their practical and aesthetic value as any plant. A beautiful flower is spoilt by an ugly pot and good food will be less enjoyable on a cheap plastic table than on a beautiful oak or stone one. Having exposed my prejudices, it is important that you choose the garden furniture *you* like and not fall into any conventional limitations of garden taste. Furnishing a garden is all about making personal choices and exercising them within your means.

First of all, you must have somewhere to sit in the garden. I have never understood why people will tolerate garden furniture that they would not dream of having inside their house. Why is it acceptable to have an ugly set of plastic chairs and table outside when you have spent time and money getting chairs and tables that you like for indoors? As I have said throughout this book, you can spoil an entire garden by one ugly or mismatched plant or object and the small garden has an unforgiving tyranny of inclusiveness in this respect. So think as carefully about your outdoor seats and tables as you do about those inside.

This does not mean that garden furniture has to be expensive. We use scaffolding planks on old painter's trestles and they look great, as well as being easy to move. I know someone who uses for a table a huge old gravestone, supported on brick piers.

Every garden, however small, must have somewhere to sit. The planting should be designed to enhance the pleasure of the sitter, as well as using the seat as a focal point.

Whatever you use needs to have weight and solidity, even if it is not fixed in one position. Although there are some advantages to mobility, it is better to identify the areas of the garden where you would like to sit, make seating there and plan the garden around it. Even a small garden can have three or four different seats to catch the sun at different times of day. Your table must have room to manoeuvre around it yet it wants to be enclosed by plants and protected from any wind with either climbers, hedges or some kind of screen. It will need to have means of drainage – as will most seats. There are few things worse than getting a sodden backside from sitting on a soaked cushion. Paving slabs make good seats, particularly if they are placed up against a wall so that you can lean back. Even a plank of wood supported by bricks works well.

If you want to go down a more conventional road and use ready-made wooden seats, try and choose oak ones. They weather beautifully, need no treatment at all and have an actual and a visual solidity. Cheaper wood can look very good when painted. Use the same colour for seats as for doors, drainpipes, gutters and handles – this ties the house and garden together and gives unity and harmony. If you do not have garden furniture you can always paint the fences. Trellis and larchlap fencing in particular tend to come in an awful shade of orange; they look much better painted some shade of green or blue or else simply white or black.

Lighting can look both good and very bad in the garden. It is certainly nice to eat outside after dark on a warm summer's night but when that darkness is broken by lurid green or red lights the atmosphere is spoiled. I prefer candles. One way to prevent candles being blown out is to put some sand in the bottom of small brown paper bags so that they do not blow around and place a lighted nightlight in each one. Lined up either side of a path or around the top of a table they will look magical, provide illumination, and stay lit for up to eight hours.

Colour is important on everything in the garden - not just plants.

Kit

GARDEN TOOLS ARE A PASSION OF MINE. I LOVE THE FACT THAT MANY HAVE REACHED A STATE OF EVOLUTIONARY PERFECTION, WHERE FUNCTION AND FORM COMBINE TO MAKE THE COMPLETELY BEAUTIFUL FUNCTIONAL OBJECT. When you have a spade, hoe or fork that gives you actual pleasure to handle and use, you will inevitably enjoy gardening more, even if you are doing banal tasks. It is the difference between chopping vegetables in the kitchen with a sharp, well-balanced knife or a blunt, flimsy one. So choose your tools with the same care that you choose your plants: there is no room for anything ugly in a small garden.

A constant problem in a small town garden is knowing where to store your tools as well, perhaps, as a wheelbarrow, a pile of empty pots, bag of compost, fertiliser and the inevitable paraphernalia of any garden. Too often the mower ends up under the stairs next to the vacuum cleaner and the fork and spade live in the corner of the kitchen. The alternative is a shed which takes up precious space – and the average garden shed is an eyesore. There is no easy answer to this problem, but I will assume that you want to keep kit down to a minimum.

The one indispensible tool in any garden that has soil is a **spade**. It should feel right in the hand and, ideally, have a stainless steel blade. If you have heavy soil this becomes an absolute necessity. A good spade will cover most digging situations but you will also need a **fork**. Make sure that this is strong and that the tines (spikes) are not too curved. With garden tools you invariably pay for what you get, so buy the best you can afford. Spades and forks come in two sizes, large and small, normally called digging and border respectively. The border tools are useful for planting in small spaces but should be bought as an addition to digging tools, not instead of them.

You must have a **hoe**. Hoes have two basic designs: one with a blade that chops the weeds and the other a Dutch hoe, with a blade that slides under them. The latter is generally more useful. Make sure that the handle is long enough and keep the blade sharp. You will also need a **rake** if you are going to sow any seeds. Round tines are better than flat ones, and make sure that it is not too wide as a smaller rake will reach those parts that other rakes just cannot reach. A wire rake, normally used to rake up moss in lawns or leaves in autumn, doubles well as a soil rake. A **wheelbarrow** is very useful, particularly if you have side access. Go for a builder's barrow, which is stronger, cheaper and looks better than any of the ordinary garden ones. They store well tipped up against a wall.

Even if you just have a window box, a **trowel** and **hand fork** will be useful. But, as with their larger equivalent, cheap ones are a waste of money and good ones are expensive. Buy a stainless steel trowel and you will use it for the rest of your life. Cheap hand forks bend pathetically easily at the join between handle and tines. A good pair of **secateurs** is essential for all pruning. They *must* be sharp, and the only way to keep them that way is to buy a pair made of good quality steel. It is a mistake to buy secateurs that are too big for your hand: always choose a pair that will fit comfortably in your pocket and are easy for you to use. While on the subject of cutting tools, a ball of tarred twine and a roll of soft green twine will cover all tying eventualities.

A **watering can** is essential and metal ones are much nicer than plastic ones, looking decorative even if left lying around – which helps the storage problem. Unless you have a tiny garden you will need a **hosepipe** as well. And if you have a hosepipe it is worth having an outside tap fitted – no, I would put it more

strongly than that – *every* garden needs an outside tap. I would say that one of the most sensible installations in a small garden would be an irrigation system. In a larger garden this gets pricey, but it would save hours of watering time in a town plot and guarantee that the garden would always look lush, without wasting any water. An irrigation system can range from a perforated pipe laid on top of the soil to highly sophisticated computer-operated systems that will run a number of different sprays and sprinklers

in sequence. The perforated pipe is simplest and probably best; it will leak water directly to the roots of plants, avoiding the waste of evaporation on leaves. It is operated from a microchip-controlled device attached to the tap which can be preset to turn the water on and off when you want it.

Finally, one of the most useful bits of kit in any garden is a **builder's bucket**. This will prove invaluable for putting weeds in as well as for carrying compost and water.

Practicalities

Plants for specific conditions

INTRODUCTION

THIS PART OF THE BOOK IS JUST A SERIES OF QUICK REFERENCES focused on the variety of specific situations that you may have in your garden and plant suggestions for them. It is not intended to be inclusive and you might find that I have omitted a very common plant or a particular favourite of yours. Like everything in this book, what is included reflects my own personal choice and opinion. Only you can decide what you like best in your own garden.

The main purpose of these lists is to encourage you to work with the conditions that you find yourself with. If your garden is overshadowed all day by other buildings, it is stupid to struggle to grow sun-loving plants. You have to make the most of the shade and limit your choice of plants to the huge variety that will relish it. If you live in an area with alkaline soil, then accept that you cannot grow rhododendrons, camellias or heathers except in containers. If you live in a frost pocket, then tender plants are not going to have an easy ride, however much care you lavish on them.

Obviously most gardens have a mixture of conditions, with shaded parts, exposed corners or even varying pH levels. By orchestrating these variations you can grow a wide range of plants and create a number of moods within the confines of a very small garden. But no small garden (and very few large ones) can have everything. Grow what wants to be there and thrives and accept the restrictions as part of the design choices that are inevitably imposed on any situation. This is the nub of my attitude to gardening: everything, from plants on the window sill to the position of a lawn, comes down to a matter of design. Once you have decided what you want to grow and where you want to grow it, then you can focus on horticulture.

Wind

WIND IS THE GARDENER'S GREATEST ENEMY. You only have to see the shape and size of trees by a blustery part of the coast, their exposed sides sliced away by the prevailing wind, to understand how important shelter is to any plant. Wind stunts all growth to a radical extent, dries leaves out quicker than sun and reduces otherwise tolerable winter temperatures to a critical level. North and eastern winds will always be cold and dry – and dangerous to all plants; a west wind will be wet and generally benign and the southern wind is always warm and dry, so potentially desiccating.

In some respects the urban gardener has a great advantage in that, generally speaking, town gardens are sheltered by neighbouring buildings. However these can also funnel wind and magnify its force and effect in a very localised way. The only solution is to create barriers that will block and filter the wind. Walls and fences will provide total protection in their lee over a distance of up to four times their height, but beyond that the wind will spill over with extra force. Trees, hedges, shrubs and even tall perennials are excellent filters for more fragile plants growing in their shade. If you are waiting for a hedge or shrubs to establish, woven hurdles are ideal and even netting will be effective in providing some protection and therefore speeding up growth.

Plants get physically knocked about and damaged by wind, especially if the wind is channelled by walls and buildings into a corner or a particular spot. Always stake and tie up tall plants and climbers and do so when they are young, and *before* they get damaged! Some plants are better than others at surviving wind and if you have an exposed garden you should choose your plants carefully until you have sufficient screening to protect the site.

TREES
Betula utilis (birch)
Sorbus aucuparia (mountain ash)

HEDGES
Carpinus betulus (hornbeam)
Fagus sylvatica (beech)
Ilex aquifolium (holly)
Thuya plicata

SHRUBS
Berberis
Euonymus
Potentilla fruticosa
Rosa rugosa
Sambucus nigra (elder)

PERENNIALS
Achillea
Astrantia major
Brunnera
Centaurea montana
Crocosmia lucifer
Euphorbia
Nepeta x *faassenii* (catmint)

ANNUALS
(On the whole the annuals that do best in exposed conditions are low-growing)
Eschscholzia californica
Limnanthes douglasii (poached-egg plant)
Verbascum 'Silver Lining'

BULBS
Crocus
Eranthis hyemalis (winter aconites)
Iris reticulata
Narcissus 'Little Gem'
Scilla

(LEFT) *Sambucus nigra* is a good shelter for less tough plants.

Cold

THERE ARE A NUMBER OF CONDITIONS WHICH MAKE FOR A COLD GARDEN, SUCH AS LACK OF DIRECT SUNLIGHT, EXPOSURE TO COLD WINDS FROM THE NORTH AND EAST, HIGH ALTITUDE, OR BEING IN A FROST LINE OR POCKET. There is nothing you can do about your geographical location, but you can and must protect the garden from cold winds, which do more harm than cold air temperatures.

Winter cold is healthy for the garden in general, killing off most pests and diseases. But an exposed garden will be slow to warm up in spring and you may have to alter your calendar of gardening tasks by as much as a month behind generalisations given in newspapers and books. I find that horticultural fleece is very effective as an insulating blanket; it can be laid over the soil before planting to warm it up as well as over young plants. It is cheap to buy and easy to put on and take off. Work hard at improving the drainage of your soil (see page 157) as sitting in cold damp soil is far worse for most plants than tolerating dry cold conditions.

Having taken all protective measures, it is pointless attempting to grow plants that will not survive or flourish in a cold spot. Reserve south-facing walls and protected west-facing sites for your tenderest plants and elsewhere grow tough species that will not mind the cold. There is a large range to choose from, of which the following are some of my favourites.

SHRUBS AND CLIMBERS
Buddleja davidii
Calluna vulgaris (acid soils only)
Clematis viticella
Lonicera periclymenum
All Alba, Gallica and species roses (other than spring-flowering ones)
Spiraea thunbergii
Wisteria floribunda

PERENNIALS
Ajuga reptans (bugle)
Echinops ritro
Geranium endressii
Geranium sanguineum
Iris sibirica
Lamium maculatum
Primula vulgaris (primrose)
Pulmonaria saccharata
Saxifraga paniculata

BULBS
Crocus
Eranthis hyemalis (winter aconites)
Galanthus (snowdrops)
Lilium regale
Muscari (grape hyacinths)
Scilla

ANNUALS
Centaurea cyanus (cornflowers)
Hesperis matronalis (double rocket)
Nigella damascena (love-in-a-mist)
Papaver rhoeas (Shirley poppies)

Warm

ANY SHELTERED TOWN GARDEN IN THE SOUTHERN PART OF BRITAIN IS LIKELY TO HAVE A MILD ENOUGH CLIMATE TO GROW A SURPRISING RANGE OF PLANTS, especially if it is facing south or west. As I make clear in the section on wind (page 153), shelter is the vital factor and should be established as quickly as possible. But once you are sure of your warm, protected site, you might as well push the boat out and garden to the limits of the climate.

All fruit will grow better and ripen sooner in a warm garden, but you could try and make the most of the benign conditions by growing fruits that rarely ripen out of doors in Britain, such as figs, peaches, oranges or lemons, apricots and nectarines, all of which need freely draining soil. The critical period for all these fruits is in spring, when they are flowering, as frost will stop the formation of fruit, so they can only be grown in a really warm, protected spot in the northern hemisphere. Strawberries will ripen quicker and taste more intense grown in a warm garden; they can be grown in a hanging basket or container.

If your garden is frost-free, bananas will grow well in summer although they will need covering in winter, but the advent of horticultural fleece has made this perfectly possible. Bananas like rich soil and lots and lots of water. Many of the more tender plants that will grow in our climate are not tropical but Mediterranean in origin. These will fare best in drier conditions, which tends to mean that they need watering less often, which is a relief.

CLIMBERS (FOR SHELTERED SOUTH WALLS ONLY)

Actinidia deliciosa (Kiwi fruit)
Clematis cirrhosa var. *balearica*
Eccremocarpus scaber
Ipomoea (morning glory)
Myrtus communis (myrtle)
Passiflora caerulea (passion flower)

TREES AND SHRUBS

Cordyline indivisa
Cupressus sempervirens (Lombardy cypress)
Eucalyptus gunnii
Gleditsia triacanthos
Dicksonia antarctica (tree fern)
Musa basjoo (banana)

PERENNIALS

Begonia sutherlandii
Canna 'Firebird'
Crinum x *powellii*
Datura cornigera
Leonotis ocymifolia
Melianthus major
Myosotidium hortensia (Chatham Island forget-me-not)
Puya aplestris

(FAR LEFT) Snowdrops do not mind the cold, wet or shade. Every home should have some.
(LEFT) Lush tropical foliage gives the illusion of a steamy climate but plants such as *Canna*, *Melianthus* and even banana will grow in a sheltered, sunny spot in a north European garden.

155

Dry

IT IS LIKELY THAT YOUR GARDEN SOIL is drier than most of its plants would like to be. This need not be a problem if you do a combination of the following things.

- Water your garden. In general it is much more effective to water less often but more thoroughly – in other words, a really good soak once a week does more good than a shower every day. The water soaks in to a greater depth and encourages the roots to penetrate further down.

- Improve the water-retention properties of the soil by adding lots of organic matter, both by digging it in and by mulching the surface with it. This will also reduce water evaporation and stop the growth of weeds – which would compete for water with the plants you want to keep.

- Remember that wind dries foliage and soil as much as lack of rain and providing shelter is an important way to reduce the demands for water made by plants.

- Choose plants that will suffer least from dry conditions and even a few that really need them to thrive. On the right is a list of plants that do well in dry conditions.

TREES AND SHRUBS
Acer campestre (field maple)
Buddleja
Ceanothus
Cistus (rock rose)
Cotoneaster
Elaeagnus
Hedera (ivy)
Juniperus (juniper)
Lavandula (lavender)
Rosa rugosa
Rosmarinus officinalis (rosemary)
Ruta graveolens (rue)
Salvia (sage)

Santolina (cotton lavender)
Thymus (thyme)

PERENNIALS
Acanthus
Achillea
Anthemis
Artemisia
Cardunculus (cardoon)
Euphorbia
Iris
Nepeta (catmint)
Papaver orientalis (oriental poppy)
Sedum

(ABOVE) *Cistus* will grow out of very dry soil or even rock as long as it has plenty of sun. (RIGHT) Dogwood will grow in most soils but is at its best in damp conditions.

Wet

YOU MIGHT HAVE WET SOIL FOR A NUMBER OF REASONS, but unless the water-table is unusually high, or you live in an area of exceptionally high rainfall, it is likely that you can improve the situation.

New houses, especially those built as part of an estate, invariably have very compacted soil as a result of machinery running over it during construction. It is common for a thin layer of topsoil to be spread over the entire garden and for this to be turfed, which looks fine for a few months. However, it is merely covering up the essential problem. Soil compaction stops the soil draining properly and makes it difficult for the tender growing tips of roots to break through, resulting in sodden ground and stunted plants. If you also have a heavy soil, like clay, then the situation goes from bad to worse.

The only answer is to dig as deeply as possible, breaking up the hard layer or 'pan', caused by compaction, and mixing in as much organic material as you possibly can. If the soil is heavy it is a good investment to spread a layer of horticultural grit 5cm (2in) deep and fork this in too. Mulch the soil as thickly as you can – up to 20cm (8in) deep if you have the material – every year and gradually you will create soil conditions that will drain well and in which roots can grow easily. If your garden is on a slope or water from neighbours' gardens is running into yours, dig a 30cm (12in) deep trench at the wettest point and put in a 15cm (6in) layer of hardcore before replacing the topsoil. This will act as a drain.

Shade and shelter will exacerbate the problem of wet soil as the lack of sun or wind slows down the drying-out process. Therefore it is a good idea to stick to plants that like wet conditions and to relish their generally lush foliage and vigorous growth. The following plants positively enjoy moist soil.

TREES AND SHRUBS
Alnus (alder)
Cornus alba (dogwood)
Pyrus communis (pear)
Salix alba (willow)
Sorbus (mountain ash)

PERENNIALS
Ajuga reptans (bugle)
Aruncus dioicus

Caltha palustris (kingcups)
Convallaria majalis (lily-of-the-valley)
Corydalis flexuosa
Darmera peltata
Hosta
Inula helenium
Iris sibirica
Ligularia
Macleaya cordata
Primula japonica

Rodgersia

ANNUALS
Limnanthes douglasii (poached-egg plant)
Mimulus (monkey flowers)
Tagetes (marigolds)

BULBS
Fritillaria
Galanthus nivalis (snowdrops)

Light

TOO MUCH SUN MIGHT HARDLY SEEM TO BE A PROBLEM IN A GARDEN, yet it does present a few limitations as to what will thrive. Clearly the trick is to make the most of your sunshine and to grow plants that at the very least would not flourish in shade. I would go further than that and plant nothing that even tolerates shade. This means that you will be expanding the range of plants as far as it will go in our climate.

Sunny situations heat up sooner than shaded ones, which makes them excellent spots for early spring flowers. Also, you can generally sow seed earlier and plants will mature quicker, provided they have sufficient water and good soil. But sunshine in itself does not mean that the air temperature will be any warmer or that you will not be exposed to winds that will dehydrate and cool plants, so do not neglect to provide shelter just because you are getting all the available sunshine. However, sunny sites usually mean hot ones which can also mean that they are dry, so enrich the soil and mulch thickly every spring to conserve moisture. If you have a very sunny patio, use it for plants as well as humans by filling it with containers, which have the advantage that they can be moved into the light to make the most of it throughout the seasons and even the day.

In the northern hemisphere any south or south-west aspect will be sunniest but bright sun early in the morning can be very damaging for tender spring-flowering plants like camellias, as any ice on the flowers from frost will act as a magnifying glass and burn delicate petals before the heat has time to defrost them. By the time the sun reaches a south aspect any frost will have melted before it receives direct sunshine.

Most vegetables and herbs relish as much sunshine as possible, as do most flowering annuals. Fruit will ripen better in sunshine and an espalier-trained pear, for example, can easily be grown against a sunny wall. See pages 60–61 for wall plants in full sunshine.

CLIMBER
Clematis armandii

PERENNIALS
Agapanthus
Argyranthemum
'Jamaica Primrose'
Canna
Eryngium

Iris unguicularis
Bearded iris
Papaver orientalis
Stachys byzantina
Yucca gloriosa

BULBS
Lilium regale
Tulipa

Dark

SHADE IS A MAJOR INFLUENCE ON URBAN GARDENS, with neighbouring buildings often obscuring the sun. This is a limitation rather than a problem and there are plenty of plants that enjoy shade and will thrive in it. There are, of course, varying degrees of shade and it is important to observe the garden at all times of the day and the year and, mentally at least, chart the shady areas. It may be that a building wholly obscures low sun in winter, early spring and late autumn, but the sun will rise above it for the rest of the year. Equally, there will be parts of your garden that are sunless for much of the day but might get an all-important burst of light for an hour or two.

Shade also comes in different qualities. Dappled shade – like that beneath a deciduous shrub or small tree – is the perfect situation for many spring flowers. Morning shade tends to be good for tender species which will relish the warmer evening sunshine, and evening shade is fine for pale-flowered plants that look best in morning light. The hardest situation to deal with is dry shade but adding plenty of compost and frequent watering will help to combat it.

TREES, SHRUBS AND CLIMBERS
Berberis
Buxus (box)
Camellia
Choisya ternata
Clematis montana
Cotoneaster
Euonymus
Hedera (ivy)
Ilex (holly)
Juniperus
Lonicera (honeysuckle)
Mahonia aquifolium
Rosa 'New Dawn'
Rosa 'Souvenir du Dr Jamain'
Rosa 'Zéphirine Drouhin'
Taxus baccata (yew)

PERENNIALS
Digitalis (foxgloves)
Many ferns
Geranium phaeum
Helleborus
Hosta
Pulmonaria

BULBS
Anemone blanda (wood anemones)
Eranthis (aconites)
Galanthus nivalis (snowdrops)

(LEFT) The globes of *Centaurea* rise above the flat flower umbels of fennel. (ABOVE) Dry shade is the hardest place to grow anything, but many ferns love it.

Acid soil

THE pH RANGE FOR SOIL RUNS FROM 3 – which you would find on a peat bog – to 8.5 for chalk. 7.0 is neutral and the optimum pH value for most plants is 6.5, which is just slightly acidic. Below 6.0 and root formation can be damaged and, as low as 4.0, many minerals are washed out and phosphates become largely unavailable. Unless the plant is specifically adapted to these conditions, it will struggle and lime-lovers will die.

Acidic soil can have its pH slightly raised by adding lime to the soil, but this must be done carefully. It should not need doing more than once every three or four years and will not alter the basic character of the soil. Mulching every year with mushroom compost will also raise the alkalinity of the soil. If your soil is peaty it will certainly be acidic and clay is often on the acidic side. If you do not want to do a pH test on your soil (and it is perfectly simple even for a non-scientist like myself), then simply look around: if you see rhododendrons and azaleas growing, then it is bound to be acidic.

If you have limey soil and you want to grow acid-loving plants then you must do so in containers or beds filled with ericaceous compost. In fact there are two groups of plants that will grow well in acidic soil: those that need the acid and those, like rhododendrons, that hate lime. But the net effect is the same.

(ABOVE) The flowers of *Meconopsis sheldonii* almost define blue. But it needs an acidic soil to prosper.

(RIGHT) Bearded irises, on the other hand, are happiest in a limey soil.

PLANTS THAT THRIVE IN ACIDIC SOIL

Acer (most maples)
Betula (birch)
Camellia
Cornus
Cotoneaster
Erica and *Calluna* (heathers and heaths)

Hammamelis (witch hazel)
Ilex (holly)
Juniperus
Lilium
Lonicera (honeysuckle)
Lupinus
Magnolia (most)

Meconopsis
Pieris
Pinus (pines)
Rhododendron (rhododendrons and azaleas)
Robinia
Trillium

Alkaline soil

ALKALINE SOIL HAS A pH (SEE PAGE 160) OF ABOVE 7.0 AND IS LIMEY. This affects gardens anywhere on the chalk belt that runs diagonally across England from Dorset to Lincolnshire. Chalk and limestone soil is rich in calcium which is quickly washed out of sandy or peaty soils, turning them acidic. Most alkaline soils over chalk or lime have good drainage but tend to be rather 'thin' and need to have lots of organic matter added to them to help them retain moisture and to improve the soil structure. They will warm up quickly in spring and therefore seeds will germinate earlier in the year than on acidic soils such as peat or clay.

Almost all flowering shrubs like lime and climbers such as clematis are very happy with it. Most vegetables and fruits prefer a slightly acidic soil and the addition of sulphur (which you can buy in pellet form) can lower the pH of your soil. Adding lots of cow manure will also increase the soil's acidity over the years. Plants growing locally that are sure indicators of alkalinity are beech, yew, flowering Japanese cherries and an absence of rhododendrons or azaleas.

PLANTS THAT LIKE LIME

Sorbus (beech)
Buddleja
Ceanothus
Clematis
Dianthus (garden pinks)
Bearded iris
Lavandula (lavender)
Primula veris (cowslips)
Pyrus salicifolia 'Pendula' (weeping pear)
Roses
Rosmarinus (rosemary)
Syringa (lilac)
Weigela

Roof gardens

A ROOF GARDEN IS ONE OF THE GREAT JOYS OF A CITY. I recall riding up 50 floors in a glass lift in San Francisco and seeing perhaps a dozen roof gardens, all at different levels, revealed to me. They seemed incredibly glamorous and beautiful.

Roof gardens have so much going for them and the first of these advantages is the delight of looking over a roofscape. There is such a feeling of liberty, of being on top of the world and escaping from grown-up reality. The second bonus is that there is always more light up there. With this extra brightness come some potential problems. A grey sky tends to suck out light and colour, so you need to create a transition, or a foreground to the sky, which on the ground comes from trees and buildings. Up on the roof you get all the sun that there is, but everything depends upon the roof's orientation. If it faces north-east it will never amount to much except on the hottest days, and will consequently hardly be used.

The second thing that makes it possible to relax on a roof is shelter from the wind. Roofs are always more exposed than gardens at ground level and wind not only chills humans but desiccates plants terribly. Evergreens are particularly vulnerable to drought, even in the middle of a cold winter. But for all the screens and wind baffles in the world, roof gardens will always need much more watering than a terrestrial garden exposed to the same rainfall and wind levels. A watering system helps, although the manual act of watering, as it represents much of the 'gardening' the owner will do, is perhaps an important part of the garden. Either way, it is essential to have a tap on the roof and to allow sufficient drainage for the water to escape.

It may sound obvious, but make sure that you have proper access to the roof, so that you can get pots, a table, chairs, trays of food and all the paraphernalia of garden life out there. The easier it is to use, the more time you will spend in it. Before you make a roof garden there are a number of practical considerations that must be attended to.

PRACTICAL CHECKLIST

- Check the orientation: if the roof is not naturally sunny and sheltered you will not use it.
- Have a survey done by a qualified engineer to verify the roof's load-bearing capacity. Many roofs are not designed to take the extra weight.
- Get the necessary planning permission. In some areas roof gardens are considered to be an additional floor.
- Consider safety. Some sort of parapet or strong barrier is essential.
- Have a tap fitted out on the roof. If you are going to be away frequently or cannot depend on help with watering in your absence, you will need to fit an irrigation system.
- Make every provision for getting all water, be it from irrigation or rainwater, off the roof as quickly and easily as possible.
- You must have wind protection. Combine this with creating privacy. It can either take the form of a general barrier surrounding the whole area, or be more specific, based around seating areas and large containers.
- Start with small plants which are much easier to get up there and less demanding on water – they will grow quickly.
- Fit the roof with some kind of lighting so that you can use it at night.

This picture proves that you do not need to be rooted in the ground to create a really colourful and diverse garden.

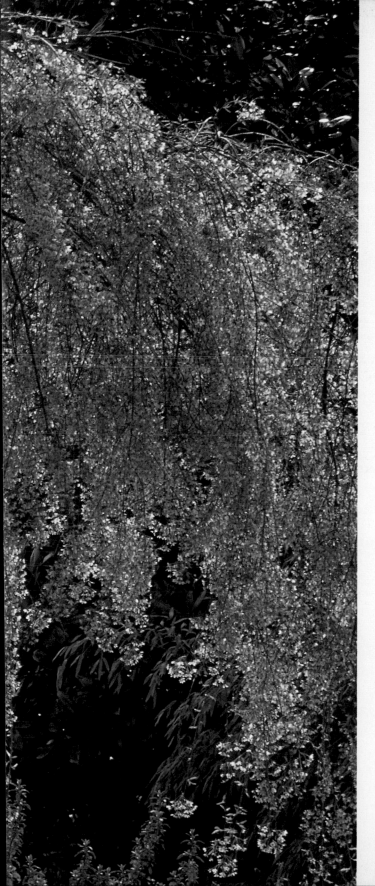

Calendar

THE FOLLOWING PAGES give a rough outline of jobs to be done at certain times of the year and plants that you might expect to be performing from month to month. This is not written in stone. Weather conditions vary from year to year and place to place and there is no norm to go by. I know that this is frustrating for the novice because what one longs for is certainty, for hard and fast rules that one can learn and apply. But I am afraid it ain't like that. On the whole, however, plants are remarkably adaptable and most gardening rules can be broken with impunity. But a general outline is always helpful and experience has taught me a few lessons which I pass on as seasonal tips.

- Try and get as much as possible of your digging and planting done before Christmas. This applies especially to deciduous trees, hedges and shrubs, as well as to any plants that you are moving.
- Mulch some time between January and May: this is the single most important annual job.
- It is better to plant or move something between August and December than between January and July.
- The best time to prune is when *you* are ready to do it, but remember that winter pruning encourages growth and summer pruning limits it.
- Do not be too anxious to get tender plants into the ground. Wait until you are certain that all frosts are over – even if that is mid-June. April and May can be very wet and cold.
- Resist being too eager to tidy the garden in late autumn. Birds and insects need the cover of dying vegetation.
- I have probably said this ten times in the book already, but whatever the season, wherever you live, cold wind is your biggest enemy. Do all you possibly can to provide protection and shelter from it.

The small weeping cherry, *Prunus subhirtella* 'Pendula Rosea', can provide flowers on its bare branches during mild intervals from autumn right through to spring, defying the normal seasonal restrictions.

January

THE START OF THE CALENDAR YEAR IS A TIME OF STASIS IN THE GARDEN. The weather is likely to get worse throughout the month, the days are very short and in truth you are likely to be outside very little. The garden is at its most naked, so it is a good time to take stock of its structure formed by evergreens, hedges, the layout of paths and borders, fences and walls and any trees that you have. If the general shape and form of the garden is not pleasing at this time of year, then you must plan to change it so that it is. The design of a garden is only as good as its bones and in January the skeleton is laid bare.

GENERAL UPKEEP

This is when you really start to value your yew and box hedges, your topiary and your hardy evergreen plants. Assess how your evergreens are working for you in the garden and make plans to carry out any changes you want. Now is not the time to transplant evergreens or to plant new ones, so you have a few months to ponder what to do.

- Provided the weather is dry enough and not frosty, now is a good time to plant any deciduous trees, climbers and shrubs.
- Dig over any ground to be planted in spring, adding whatever organic material you can and leaving the soil in large clumps (if you prepare the final surface now, it will compact in the rain and have to be redug).

BULBS

Depending on the weather, winter aconites and the first of the snowdrops should come out this month. There is nothing to do other than enjoy them!

IN FULL FLOWER

Eranthis hyemalis (winter aconites)
Iris histrioides

PERENNIALS

- Frost can lift the roots of plants that are not fully established, so check on this and tread the roots down around the plant if they seemed to have risen up above ground level.
- Hellebores are the stars of the winter garden and they are beginning to come into flower. Remove the old leaves as soon as the new ones start to appear and burn them as they are very slow to rot and can spread disease.
- Winter pansies are beginning to flower in sheltered positions.

IN FULL FLOWER

Helleborus niger (Christmas rose)
Iris unguicularis
Viola (winter pansies)

SHRUBS

- Shake any snow from evergreens as it can very easily snap the branches.
- Plant any deciduous shrubs (and trees) you buy if the weather is dry enough, making sure you dig a really generous hole and give them lots of goodness. Leave evergreens until spring.
- There is a range of winter-flowering shrubs that are fully in flower throughout January and February and which every garden should have, if only to cheer the spirits a little. Most of them make excellent cut flowers

and a little vase of sweetly scented flowers on a bare stem does a lot to dispel midwinter gloom.

IN FULL FLOWER

Chimonanthus praecox (winter sweet)
Cornus alba sibirica (dogwood)
Erica carnea (heathers)
Lonicera fragrantissima (winter honeysuckle)
Skimmia japonica
Viburnum bodnantense

CLIMBERS

- Tie in all climbers if you have not done so already, to prevent wind damage. Check trellis and wire supports in readiness for new growth in spring.

CONTAINERS

Winter is when containers will be put to a true test of their drainage. If plants have to sit in cold, sodden soil for days on end they will at best be droopy and more likely will die. If the soil does seem to be overly wet, it is perfectly reasonable to take the plants out, empty the soil, put in extra drainage, like crocks, grit or polystyrene chips, add horticultural grit to the compost and replant the whole container. Cover the surface with a layer of grit to stop the leaves sitting in winter wet.

The chunkiness of *Skimmia reevesiana* and its bright red berries is set against the delicacy of snowdrops.

GOOD ENOUGH TO EAT

- *Herbs* Rosemary, sage, parsley and thyme should still be available for picking.
- *Vegetables* Parsnips, cabbage, chard and beetroot will all be fine in the ground.
- *Salads* Rocket, mizuna and lamb's lettuce should also be growing well. Cover salad plants with a cloche or fleece if it is very cold.

February

FEBRUARY USUALLY HAS THE VERY WORST WEATHER OF THE YEAR, but I like it. The days are noticeably lengthening, the birds start singing – February 14th is the medieval feast of the birds, when traditionally they chose their mates, hence our St Valentine's Day – and, above all, there is just a glimmer of promise of the spring to come. But do not be seduced by the occasional warm or bright day. This is still very much midwinter and it is certain there will be more harsh weather to come.

GENERAL UPKEEP

- Concentrate your energies on preparing your soil if you have not done so by now and planting any deciduous trees, hedges and shrubs by the end of the month.
- If the weather is freakishly warm the grass will start to grow. Resist the temptation to cut it. Any extra growth will protect it from the cold weather that will follow as sure as night follows day.
- Try and finish any work on paths, walls, patios, sheds, fences or trellis that you may want to do.

BULBS

The bulb season is now entering its prime and in a sheltered garden bulbs should be performing well. Keep a record of what is looking good and what might be moved or added to; ideally, take photographs to remind you.

- Snowdrops and aconites can be divided or moved, either in flower or immediately after flowering. Both like shady, slightly moist sites in winter, although they do not mind dry summers.

IN FULL FLOWER

Crocus
Galanthus nivalis (snowdrops)
Iris histrioides
Iris reticulata
Narcissus 'February Gold'
Scilla bifolia

ANNUALS

- Sow half-hardy annuals at the end of the month if you have a greenhouse or cold frame or even a sunny window sill.

PERENNIALS

Enjoy hellebores in this their season. The longer I garden the more pleasure I get from them, especially the humblest and easiest, the Lenten rose (*Helleborus orientalis* and all its cultivars). The first primroses will be flowering and they are the best sign of spring there is. Pulmonarias also begin to come into flower.

IN FULL FLOWER

Helleborus orientalis (Lenten rose)
Helleborus foetidus (stinking hellebore)
Helleborus argutifolius (Corsican hellebore)

SHRUBS

This is the best month for winter-flowering shrubs, although in a mild year they are starting to put on leaf and will finish flowering by the end of the month. Camellias will be beginning to flower but will need protection from hard frost; horticultural fleece is ideal for this.

IN FULL FLOWER

Camellia
Cornus
Daphne mezereum
Garrya elliptica

Hamamelis mollis (witch hazel)
Lonicera fragrantissima (winter honeysuckle)
Mahonia japonica
Viburnum farreri
Viburnum tinus

TREES

The sap is rising in trees and this is particularly visible with birches. The best flowering tree (practically the only one) is the winter-flowering cherry *(Prunus* x *subhirtella* 'Autumnalis').

- Finish any pruning of deciduous trees. Do not paint the wounds but make sure you leave a slight stub which has tissue that will heal over naturally.

AT THEIR BEST
Alnus and *Corylus* (alders and hazel) for their catkins
Prunus x *subhirtella* 'Autumnalis'

CLIMBERS

The earliest clematis, *C. cirrhosa* var. *balearica*, is in flower and is ideal for a sheltered warm wall. Winter-flowering jasmine will grow in deep shade and has lovely buttery flowers.

- Prune winter jasmine back tight to the wall immediately after flowering at the end of the month.

AT THEIR BEST
Clematis cirrhosa var. *balearica*
Jasminum nudiflorum (winter-flowering jasmine)

CONTAINERS

Alpines love cold, bright weather, plenty of water and can take any amount of cold and wet as long as they have very, very good drainage. I mix horticultural grit with potting compost in a 50:50 ratio and everything seems to grow well in it. Ideally they should be in a sunny but sheltered position.

IN FULL FLOWER
Gentiana (dwarf gentians)
Saxifraga
Viola

GOOD ENOUGH TO EAT
- *Herbs* Split chives and replant. They should begin to show new growth this month.
- *Vegetables* If you have space, sow broad beans and early lettuce under cloches.

The winter aconite, *Eranthus hyemalis*.

March

THIS IS THE START OF THE GARDENING SEASON and, if the weather is mild, can be one of the busiest months of the year. However, go by the weather and the conditions in your garden, not by the calendar. If the soil is still wet and cold, wait until it is ready – even if you are seemingly behind the horticultural run of things. A good rule is that if the soil sticks to your shoes when you walk on it, then it is too wet to work or plant into. If it feels cold and clammy to the touch, then it is too early to sow seeds.

Although the weather can still be harsh, this is only in bursts and for gardeners the longer days and increasing warmth is really exciting. You can almost sense the life pulsing through the soil. If the weather is unusually mild you will find many things coming into leaf and flower and running the risk of damage from later frosts. Good wind protection can stop this and covering shrubs and climbers with a veil of horticultural fleece is usually all the emergency protection needed.

GENERAL UPKEEP
- Mulch the bare ground as soon as you can with a thick layer of organic material: mushroom compost is ideal.
- Weed first, taking care to remove all perennial weeds such as bindweed, couch grass, nettles, docks or thistles. If you can get the worst of your weeds cleared now, it will be much easier to stay on top of them for the rest of the year.
- Spring-clean lawns by scratching them vigorously with a wire rake to remove any thatch (dead roots) and moss. Aerate with a fork, sticking it in as deep as possible all over.
- Cut the grass with the blades set high, just taking the top off to a uniform length. Do not cut too short.

BULBS
- Dead-head daffodils as they finish flowering but do not remove any leaves.
- Plant summer-flowering bulbs such as lilies, dahlias, gladioli and alliums.

IN FULL FLOWER
Erythronium
Leucojum vernum (spring snowflakes)
Muscari (grape hyacinths)
Narcissus (daffodils)
Scilla
Tulipa (early tulips)

ANNUALS
- Prepare the soil by raking it finely and sow hardy annuals such as nigella, Shirley poppies and calendulas outside.

PERENNIALS
- Plant herbaceous perennials and water plants in well, even if rain is likely.
- Divide and replant any that have become too big or that you wish to spread.
- Sprinkle bonemeal around each plant and rake lightly into the soil.

IN FULL FLOWER
All hellebores flowering in February (see page 168) should keep on thriving till the end of March.

Bergenia
Primula vulgaris (primroses)
Polyanthus
Pulmonaria
Viola (pansies)

SHRUBS

Many shrubs are bursting into flower, with the magnolias especially dramatic.

- Prune roses where necessary: hybrid Tea roses should be cut hard to healthy buds, but shrub roses need no pruning other than a light trim and climbing roses should be left alone.
- Prune buddleja hard down to low, healthy leaves and prune cornus hard as it develops leaves, to encourage bright new growth for next winter.

IN FULL FLOWER

Camellia

Chaenomeles (flowering quince)

Daphne mezereum

Eric carnea and *E. arborea*

Forsythia

Magnolia x *soulangiana*

Magnolia stellata

Pieris

Rhododendron

Ribes

Viburnum tinus

TREES

Early blossom should be appearing now. Plant any deciduous trees as soon as possible this month and water in very well.

AT THEIR BEST

Prunus x *domestica* (damson)

Prunus spinosa (blackthorn)

CLIMBERS

- Plant all climbers this month.
- Prune all late-flowering (after end of June) clematis down to the lowest healthy bud.

AT THEIR BEST

Clematis cirrhosa var. *balearica*

GOOD ENOUGH TO EAT

- *Herbs* Prune sage back to healthy leaves near the base of the shrub to stop it becoming straggly.
- *Vegetables* Sow carrots, parsnips, lettuce, spinach, beans and peas if the ground is dry enough to prepare a crumbly seedbed.
- Sow new potatoes.
- Plant onion sets and shallots.

Crocus open out to take in as much winter sunshine as possible.

April

APRIL'S WEATHER CHANGES WITH THE UNPREDICTABILITY OF A TWO-YEAR OLD'S MOOD. One moment it is hot and the next snowing or pouring with rain. The showers are exactly what the garden needs – ideally with warm spells in between. In consequence everything will grow this month. The leaves start to burst on trees and hedges and perennials push out their first leaves from the bare ground. Do not plant out tender perennials or vegetables until next month, however fine the weather seems. The risk of frost is too real. The days are stretching out and there is time to be spent out of doors in the evenings, which dramatically increases the amount of work that can be achieved this month. Try and eat some meals outside if at all possible.

GENERAL UPKEEP

A busy month, getting as much planted, weeded and actively growing as possible. Any time spent in the garden this month will reap dividends later in the summer and save work then, too.

- April is a very good month to make a lawn, either by turf or seed (see page 28).
- Continue cutting established grass in dry weather, but no more than once a week and not as short as its final summer length until all risk of frost is past.
- Feed the lawn with a general fertiliser.

BULBS

April is the month of the tulip, which can just as easily be grown in pots as in the garden.

- Keep watering bulbs in pots after they flower until the leaves die back: this will improve next year's flowers.

IN FULL FLOWER

Anemone
Cyclamen repandum
Fritillaria
Hyacinthus
Narcissus
Trillium
Tulipa

ANNUALS

- Keep sowing hardy annuals and prick out any that were sown into seed trays last month.
- Plant out sweet peas into containers or the open ground with their supports in place.

IN FULL FLOWER

Cheiranthus cheiri (wallflowers)
Lunaria annua (honesty)
Myosotis (forget-me-nots)

PERENNIALS

- The work of planting continues.
- Stake tall perennials like delphiniums now so that they can be tied in as they grow.
- Hostas are appearing from the bare soil and the new furled-up leaves are very delicious to slugs and snails: sprinkle grit around the plants to keep them at bay.

IN FULL FLOWER

Aubretia
Brunnera macrophylla
Doronicum (leopard's bane)
Polygonatum x *hybridum* (Solomon's seal)
Primula
Pulsatilla vulgaris
Viola

SHRUBS

April is the best month for planting or transplanting evergreen trees and shrubs. The roots are actively growing so will cope with the respirational demands of the plant. Water well after planting and make sure they do not dry out for the rest of the summer.

IN FULL FLOWER

Choisya ternata
Forsythia
Magnolia
Osmanthus delavayi
Pieris
Rhododendron
Skimmia japonica
Spiraea
Viburnum burkwoodii

TREES

All the fruit trees come into blossom and, with the exception of ash and oak, which are both late into leaf, most deciduous trees are putting out leaves daily.

AT THEIR BEST

Acer (maple)
Malus (crab apple)
Prunus (cherries and plums)

CLIMBERS

● Keep planting pot-grown climbers.

AT THEIR BEST

Abelia lobata
Clematis alpina
Clematis armandii

GOOD ENOUGH TO EAT

● *Herbs* Rosemary, mint, parsley, marjoram, thyme, sage, lemon balm and angelica are all growing well. Lovage and fennel are putting out leaves.

● *Vegetables* Sow as much as possible of the hardy vegetables, but wait until next month for beans, tomatoes and sweetcorn, which will not survive frost.

● This is the bleakest time of the year for vegetables, but you may be able to harvest spring greens, rocket, perhaps a few early spinach and lettuce if they were sown early and it has been very mild.

Some bulbs hint at spring or better weather to come but tulips are the real thing. When they open it confirms that spring is really here. This one has a name - 'Flaming Parrot' - almost as good as its flower.

May

MAY IS MY FAVOURITE MONTH. It arrives in spring and ends in summer and although the weather can still be cold, by the middle of the month any risk of frost is over. Everything is growing very fast, and the predominant flowers are on those plants originating in woodland that can be planted in some shade because they have evolved to flower before the leaf canopy on the trees becomes too dense. Above all, May is the month of blossom which is a sound enough reason for every garden to have a flowering fruit tree. It is good to plant as much as possible early in the month so that the roots can get established before too many demands are made by the emerging leaves, but almost anything you put in the ground this month will grow well provided it is watered sufficiently.

GENERAL UPKEEP
- Keep weeding little and often.
- Mulch all bare soil with a thick layer of organic material such as well-rotted compost (but *not* fresh manure).
- Water all newly planted hedges and shrubs weekly.
- If starting work on a new, overgrown garden, spray with 'Roundup' on a dry, windless day.
- Cut lawns weekly.

BULBS
- Cut off the dead heads of daffodils and tulips but leave their leaves to die back naturally.
- Plant out tender bulbs such as lilies and dahlias.

IN FULL FLOWER
Allium
Hyacinthoides non-scripta (bluebells)
Scilla
Tulipa

ANNUALS
- Buy and plant out annuals such as tobacco plants, morning glory, nasturtiums and marigolds.
- Sow more poppy seeds.

IN FULL FLOWER
Centaurea *cyanus* (cornflowers)

Cheiranthus cheiri (wallflowers)
Hesperis matronalis (sweet rocket)
Lunaria (honesty)
Myosotis (forget-me-nots)
Nigella (love-in-a-mist)
Papaver (poppies)

PERENNIALS
- Keep planting to fill the gaps.
- Stake herbaceous plants before they grow too tall.

IN FULL FLOWER
Aquilegia (columbines)
Dicentra spectabilis
Euphorbia griffithii, *E. wulfenii*
Geranium endressii
Geum coccineum (avens)
Bearded iris
Lupinus

Nepeta (catmint)
Paeonia
Polygonatum x *hybridum* (Solomon's seal)
Pulsatilla vulgaris (Pasque flower)
Viola 'Penny Black'

SHRUBS
- Prune forsythia after flowering.
- Dig up ribes and throw it away.

IN FULL FLOWER
Ceanothus
Deutzia
Philadelphus (mock orange)
Rhododendron (acid soil only)

Rosa 'Cantabrigiensis'
Rosa 'Nevada'
Rosa primula
Syringa (lilac)

TREES

- If you plant any tree between now and November, give it at least 10 litres (2 gallons) of water once a week.

AT THEIR BEST

Acer (maple)	*Prunus* (cherry)
Amelanchier	*Pyrus* (pear)
Crataegus (hawthorn)	*Robinia pseudoacacia*
Laburnum	*Sambucus* (elder)
Malus (apple)	*Sorbus* (whitebeam)

CLIMBERS

- Prune *Clematis montana* immediately after flowering, but only to restrict growth.
- Tie in the new growth of all climbers with soft twine.

AT THEIR BEST

Clematis alpina	*Lonicera periclymenum*
Clematis macropetala	(honeysuckle)
Clematis montana	*Rosa xanthina* 'Canary Bird'
Many large-flowered clematis	*Wisteria sinensis*

FOLIAGE PLANTS

- Plant evergreens at the beginning of the month and keep watered.
- Clip box hedges and topiary at the end of the month.

IN FULL LEAF

Artemisia vulgaris	New growth of grasses such as
Geranium 'Ann Folkard'	*Carex, Miscanthus* and *Cortaderia*
Lamium album	*Corylus maxima* 'Purpurea'
New growth of hostas, especially *H. sieboldiana*	(purple-leaved hazel)

CONTAINERS

- Clean out early bulbs (put them into a spare pot so the leaves can die back in their own time) and plant up pots and window boxes with summer bedding.
- Plant (or sow seed of) runner beans in large pot with bamboo-wigwam to support growth.

IN FULL FLOWER

Digitalis (dwarf foxgloves)	*Myosotis* (forget-me-nots)
Iris reticulata	*Scilla sibirica*
Matthiola	Lily-flowered tulips

GOOD ENOUGH TO EAT

- *Herbs* Sow parsley, dill, fennel and sweet marjoram. Plant basil in sunny spot.
- Pick chives, mint, rosemary, sage and thyme.
- *Salads* Sow small amounts of lettuce, spinach, rocket, chicory and endive at 10-day intervals.
- Radishes, lettuces, rocket, spinach and baby carrots should be ready for picking if under glass.

The field poppy, *Papaver rhoeas*.

June

JUNE HAS MORE SUNSHINE THAN ANY OTHER MONTH, if not the most heat, so everything will be growing faster than at any other season. Much of this growth is foliage and at no other time of the year is it so vibrantly, lushly green. The weather can be chilly, but any danger of frost in towns is past, so tender plants can be planted in confidence. Take note of what is doing well and pictures too, if you can, so that you can start work for this time next year in a few months time.

GENERAL UPKEEP
- Water regularly in dry weather, remembering that a good weekly soak is better than a daily drizzle.
- Keep on top of the weeds by not letting them seed.
- Lawns should be cut weekly, a little longer than is normal. They will look much better for the extra length.

BULBS
Spring bulbs will be over but their leaves will linger on. Resist all urges to tidy them and do not cut them back this month.

IN FULL FLOWER
Allium   *Lilium martagon*
Iris   *Lilium regale*

ANNUALS
Annuals are starting to come into flower, ahead of the main body of perennial flowers.

- Dead-head as much as you can and keep sowing seed to maintain successional flowering through to autumn.
- Clear away spring annuals such as forget-me-nots (do not worry about losing plants – they self-seed).
- Sow biennials such as foxgloves and wallflowers ready for next spring.

IN FULL FLOWER
Alyssum
Antirrhinum (snapdragons)
Calceolaria
Campanula (Canterbury bells)
Dianthus barbatus (sweet Williams)
Lathyrus (sweet peas)
Limnanthes douglasii (poached-egg plant)
Lobelia
Papaver (poppies)
Pelargonium
Tropaeolum (nasturtiums)

PERENNIALS
It is very important to keep perennials weeded this month and to stake and tie them as they grow rather than after they collapse.

IN FULL FLOWER
Acanthus mollis   *Geranium*
Achillea   *Iris sibirica*
Anchusa   *Lupinus*
Aquilegia (columbines)   *Paeonia* (peonies)
Aruncus   *Papaver orientale* (oriental
Astrantia   poppies)
Campanula   *Saxifraga umbrosa* (London
Delphinium   pride)
Dianthus (pinks)   *Tradescantia virginiana*
Dicentra spectabilis   *Trollius*

SHRUBS
The list of shrubs flowering in June is enormous. With careful planning these can provide the floriferous link between the last of the bulbs and the bulk of perennial flowers. Best by far are the old shrub roses, which are superb all month.

- Dead-head roses as they fade: this involves cutting back to a leaf or bud, not just pulling off faded petals.

IN FULL FLOWER

Buddleja alternifolia
Ceanothus dentatus
Cistus
Cotoneaster
Deutzia
Hebe
Kolkwitzia amabilis
Philadelphus
Potentilla fruticosa
Pyracantha
All shrub roses
Weigela

TREES

Water newly planted trees, giving two large bucketfuls each week.

AT THEIR BEST

Aesculus hippocastanum (horse chestnut)
Fraxinus (ash)
Robinia
Sorbus

CLIMBERS

- Keep picking sweet peas to encourage new growth.

AT THEIR BEST

All early-flowering clematis, such as *C.* 'Nelly Moser' and *C.* x *durandii*
Hydrangea petiolaris (climbing hydrangea)
Jasminum officinale (jasmine)
Lonicera (honeysuckle)
All climbing roses (by end of month)
Wisteria sinensis

CONTAINERS

- Place tougher house plants like Citrus and scented-leaved geraniums outside.
- Water containers regularly.
- Plant up hanging baskets and water twice a day in hot spells.

GOOD ENOUGH TO EAT

- *Herbs* Plant out basil plants in the herb garden.
- *Vegetables* Plant runner beans and dwarf French beans.
- Plant outdoor tomatoes.
- *Fruit* Net fruit against birds and watch out for slugs.
- *Salads* Sow lettuce every two weeks to get a steady supply of young plants.

Nigella often seeds itself, flowering in early summer.

July

JULY IS GENERALLY THE WARMEST MONTH – mainly because the nights cool down less than at any other time of the year. It is a month when you should be reaping the harvest of the work you have put into the garden, which is not to say that there are no jobs to do but that for a few weeks maintenance is more important than forward planning. Much of the preparatory work of winter and spring is done so that you might fully enjoy this midsummer season.

GENERAL UPKEEP
- Dead-heading will prolong the flowering season, as well as making the garden look better.
- Watering is likely to be very important this month. Stick to the general principles of giving things a really good soak once a week, rather than a daily shower, and make sure you direct the water to where it matters – the roots, not the leaves.
- Lawns might need watering. As with any other plant, give it a really good soak so that the water sinks in deeply rather than a light spray. Trim the lawn edges.

BULBS
- Plant autumn-flowering crocus (*C. speciosus* and *C. sativus*) and colchicums.
- Cut back and tidy leaves of tulips and daffodils.

IN FULL FLOWER
Galtonia candicans
Gladiolus
Lilium

ANNUALS
Tender annuals come into their own this month, providing the brightest colour in the garden.

- Keep picking sweet peas so they will produce fresh flowers all summer – otherwise they set seed and stop flowering.

- Sow wallflowers, foxgloves and Canterbury bells for flowering next year.

IN FULL FLOWER
Ageratum	*Eshscholzia* (Californian
Alyssum	poppies)
Antirrhinum (snapdragons)	*Lathyrus* (sweet peas)
Calceolaria	*Limnanthes douglasii*
Calendula (marigolds)	*Lobelia*
Dianthus (pinks)	*Oenothera* (evening primrose)
Dianthus barbatus (sweet	*Papaver* (poppies)
Williams)	*Pelargonium*
Digitalis (foxgloves)	*Petunia*

PERENNIALS
- Lift June-flowering irises and divide, replanting so that the rhizomes stand clear of the soil. Trim the leaves to 15cm (6in) to stop the roots being rocked before they establish secure new growth.

IN FULL FLOWER
Acanthus mollis	*Geranium*
Achillea	*Hemerocallis* (day lily)
Anchusa	*Hosta*
Aruncus	*Inula*
Astrantia	*Lavatera*
Campanula (Canterbury bells)	*Macleaya*
Delphinium	*Rudbeckia*
Eryngium	*Verbascum*

Shrubs

- Roses need dead-heading. Do not worry about aphids or blackspot – they rarely harm the flowers and the garden will sort itself out over the course of the summer with a predator naturally dealing with any infestation. If you are growing prize roses then you will not be reading this book.

In full flower

Ceanothus	*Lavandula*
Cistus	*Phlomis fruticosa*
Escallonia	*Potentilla fruticosa*
Hebe	All shrub roses
Hydrangea	*Spiraea*
Hypericum	*Vinca*

Trees

- Prune plums and cherries now as this reduces risk of silver leaf disease. Pruning should only be for convenience – it is not necessary for the good of the crop or the health of the plant.
- Trim deciduous hedges. Beech and hornbeam will grow new leaves after cutting which will turn a delicious russet colour and stay on the plants all winter. After cutting, weed the base of hedges and feed with bonemeal before giving a long soak.

Climbers

Tie in new clematis shoots to stop them getting top-heavy and falling back down over themselves.

At their best

All hybrid clematis	*Hydrangea petiolaris*
Jasminum officinale	*Lonicera* (honeysuckle)
(jasmine)	All climbing roses

Containers

- Hanging baskets might need watering twice a day now – especially if they are in an exposed position.

Good enough to eat

- *Herbs* Sow more parsley for autumn and winter use.
- *Vegetables* Weed all vegetables carefully as weeds take a lot of water.
- Plant a block of leeks – they look great and taste fine.
- *Fruit* Strawberries, gooseberries and all currants will be ripe and ready for harvest and will need protection from birds.
- *Salads* Sow lettuce at 10-day intervals for regular supply; sow in a site shaded from afternoon sun. You might find lettuce bolting almost before it is ready to pick: this is due to lack of water and too much heat. Keep lettuce well watered.

Sweet peas need plenty of water and goodness but are worth any amount of extra care, providing bunches of the best cut flower that there is.

August

IF YOU GO ON HOLIDAY IN AUGUST you might well return to find long grass, weeds and potentially dead plants in containers that have been unwatered for a fortnight. The latter is bad news, but other things can easily be put to rights and in a way this heralds a new phase of the year. So don't worry about it. Although the days are hotter than ever, the evenings are drawing in and getting noticeably cooler. A hot, wet August can encourage fungal infections and moulds and a hot, dry August a plague of wasps and other insects. Though wasps are bad for people, they are good for gardens as they eat other, more harmful insects.

GENERAL UPKEEP
Although it may feel like the peak time of year, August is the month when the organised gardener starts preparing for next summer. Take stock of what looks good this year and what has not worked so well.

- Move plants freely but be sure to water them very thoroughly before and after transplanting.
- Keep on top of weeds and enjoy summer while it lasts.
- The second half of August is a good time to sow grass seed: the ground is warm but the cool nights always bring dew, which keeps the seed moist. It should grow fast and establish healthy roots before winter and be a perfect lawn by next spring.

BULBS
- Start planting spring bulbs from mid-August: put them in at a depth of at least twice their own height.

IN FULL FLOWER
Crocosmia
Gladiolus
Lilium

ANNUALS
Sunflowers are at their best in August, in all their different guises.

- Cut back violas and pansies to encourage new growth.

IN FULL FLOWER

Ageratum	*Helianthus* (sunflowers)
Calendula (marigolds)	*Helichrysum*
Cosmos	*Lavatera trimestris*
Dianthus (pinks)	*Nicotiana* (tobacco plants)
Digitalis (foxgloves)	*Pelargonium*
Eshscholzia (Californian poppies)	*Scabiosa atropurpurea*
	Tropaeolum (nasturtiums)

PERENNIALS
August can be a good month for moving plants and preparing the borders for next year, as many of the earlier perennials will have stopped growing and can be safely moved. By doing it now you will get a feel for the space they occupy and the effect they will have. But always water them before and after moving and expect them to slump for a week or so.

IN FULL FLOWER

Acanthus	*Hemerocallis*
Alcea (hollyhocks)	*Hosta*
Aster	*Inula*
Astilbe	*Lavatera*
Astrantia major	*Lychnis coronaria*
Chrysanthemum	*Macleaya*
Dahlia	*Monarda*
Echinops	*Phlox paniculata*
Eupatorium	*Rudbeckia*
Filipendula	*Solidago*
Gypsophila paniculata	*Verbascum*

SHRUBS

- Trim back lavender, cutting off finished flower stems, but do not cut into old wood.
- August is traditionally the time to cut hedges and certainly the best time to clip evergreen hedges such as yew, holly, laurel or cypress.

IN FULL FLOWER

Buddleja

Ceanothus (deciduous forms)

Cistus

Clerodendron

Cotinus

Escallonia

Hebe

Hydrangea paniculata

Hypericum

Lavandula

Magnolia grandiflora

Potentilla fruticosa

Bourbon and hybrid perpetual roses

Vinca

TREES

Trees in August can look a little dowdy and jaded. Keep them well watered, especially trees planted this year.

CLIMBERS

- Prune wisteria, cutting back new growth to three leaves from their base. Prune rambler roses after flowering to restrict them in size.

AT THEIR BEST

Clematis Jackmanii group

Hydrangea petiolaris

Lonicera (honeysuckle)

Solanum crispum

Climbing roses

Tropaeolum speciosum

CONTAINERS

- Dead-head flowers and keep watering as necessary.
- If you go away, group all pots together in the shade to help moisture loss.

GOOD ENOUGH TO EAT

- *Herbs* The herb garden should be in its prime.
- *Vegetables* This is the beginning of the main harvest season of vegetables. Tomatoes will be ripening and beans coming through.

Late summer is a season of powerful colours. The English marigold, *Calendula officinalis*, is no exception, as rich an orange as any flower.

September

THE DAYS ARE DRAWING IN AND BY THE END OF THE MONTH there is a distinct autumnal cast to the light, but on the whole September is a wonderful month in the garden. It is the month of ripening, the season of harvest and you should enjoy it as such before the year really does wind to a close. The flower borders are full of rich, strong colours and in some ways at their best, while herbs and vegetables are still growing strongly.

GENERAL UPKEEP

September is the last month when you are guaranteed some good weather, so make the most of warm days. It is also the last month of the year when there is enough daylight to work outside in the evening, so use it!

- Do not let up on the weeding as the weeds will be setting seed as vigorously as the plants you wish to keep.
- September is the best time to sow grass seed as the seeds germinate fast and establish roots before winter. The grass keeps growing through till Christmas but is unlikely to dry out in the autumn. But do not delay – get on with the job as soon as possible this month and you will have a good lawn by next spring. Keep cutting established grass but do not leave clippings on the ground.

BULBS

Continue planting spring bulbs, aiming to have them all in the ground by the end of the month. Lilies should still be flowering but dahlias and the autumn-flowering crocuses are the bulb stars of the month.

IN FULL FLOWER

Colchicum

Crinum x *powellii*

Crocus speciosus, C. sativus

Cyclamen purpurascens, C. europaeum

Dahlia

Gladiolus

Oriental lilies

ANNUALS

Many annuals will go on producing flowers until the first frosts, especially if you have been dead-heading over the summer.

IN FULL FLOWER

Helianthus (sunflowers)

Oenothera biennis (evening primrose)

PERENNIALS

I love the late summer border, full of burgundies, oranges and purples. The Michaelmas daisies (Aster) come into flower this month, after a long summer of anonymous foliage. They range from the lovely to the horrible, so choose carefully before planting.

IN FULL FLOWER

Aster

Chrysanthemum

Eupatorium purpureum

Helianthus (perennial sunflowers)

Hosta

Inula

Ligularia

Penstemon

Salvia

Thalictrum

Verbena bonariensis

SHRUBS

Shrub roses often make a second flush of flowers in late summer. The berries of berberis and cotoneaster are showing and are usually left by the birds this month.

- September is a very good time for planting all evergreens, such as yew, box, holly and Portuguese laurel.

IN FULL FLOWER

Erica (acidic soil only)
Fuchsia
Hydrangea

TREES

By the end of the month leaves are turning yellow, especially if late August and early September had hot weather.

AT THEIR BEST

Aesculus hippocastanum (horse chestnut for the conkers)
Betula (birch are one of the first to turn colour)

CLIMBERS

Prune rambler roses, remembering that they need pruning only to control their growth rather than to encourage flowers.

AT THEIR BEST

Many of the late-flowering clematis will be producing masses of flowers, such as the hybrids 'Gipsy Queen', 'Etoile Violette', 'Perle d'Azur', and 'Ville de Lyon' and the species clematis, *C. jackmanii, C. flammula, C. durandii* and *C. viticella.*

CONTAINERS

- Plant spring bulbs in pots. Put them sufficiently deep to leave room to plant winter-flowering plants (such as winter pansies) over the top of them.

GOOD ENOUGH TO EAT

September for me is the month of pears, and just one perfectly ripe pear picked from the garden is worth the space of a pear tree, so exquisite is the experience. Otherwise herbs and vegetables are still growing well, especially the vegetables, which prefer the warm days and cool nights to the higher temperatures of midsummer.

- *Vegetables* Keep picking beans to encourage more growth.
- *Salads* Sow lettuce such as rocket, lamb's lettuce, mizuna and winter density for autumn and winter picking.

Helenium 'Moorhelm Beauty' has wonderful rust-coloured petals in late summer.

October

I AM ALWAYS SURPRISED AT HOW SLOWLY THE AUTUMN SEASON CREEPS IN, yet by the end of this month it is always unequivocally autumn. The leaves are falling, flowers are becoming fewer and the grass has adopted that curious tussocky texture. It is good to try and eat a few more meals outside in the autumnal sunshine, even if the air is cooler and you have to wear a coat or jersey.

GENERAL UPKEEP

Unless the season is unusually cold, the ground will still be warm, so it is a good time for planting and sowing seeds. Try and go into winter with the garden free of weeds.

- Raise the blades on your mower and, however warm the weather might be, resist the temptation to cut the grass too short. You want to leave it 2.5cm (1in) long over winter.

BULBS

- It is not too late to plant spring bulbs, but this should take priority. Plant tulips and lilies now.
- Lift any dahlia tubers, cut off the top growth and store in a dry, frost-free place over winter.

IN FULL FLOWER

Colchicum
Crocus (autumn-flowering)
Cyclamen neapolitanum
Nerine bowdenii

ANNUALS

- Sow sweet peas in pots and hardy annuals where you want them to grow next spring.
- Plant wallflowers, forget-me-nots and polyanthus in their positions for next spring.

PERENNIALS

The perennial borders are largely influenced by frost, in so far as they can still look good well into the month but a series of frosts will make them die back very fast.

- Dig any new borders to be planted and move existing plants, splitting them as you go to encourage vigorous new growth next spring.

IN FULL FLOWER

Aster novae-angliae
Aster novi-belgii
Helianthus (sunflowers)
Kniphofia
Liriope spicata
Sedum spectabile

SHRUBS

October is the month when berries have a chance to shine before the birds eat them all up. Heathers (for those that like them) start their winter flowering.

IN BERRY

Callicarpa
Celastrus
Cotoneaster
Euonymus europaeus
Ilex (holly)
Pyracantha

TREES

This is obviously the season of leaf colour. The trees and shrubs listed below are all suitable for a small garden and have superb autumnal colour.

- Plant all deciduous trees and hedges, even though most will still have their leaves. If they can establish good root growth before new leaves appear next spring they will grow much stronger.

AT THEIR BEST

Acer (maple)
Betula (birch)
Carpinus betulus (hornbeam)
Crataegus (hawthorn)
Fagus sylvatica (beech)
Malus (crab apple)
Prunus sargentii
Sorbus (mountain ash, whitebeam)
Stuartia

CLIMBERS

A few climbers have dramatic autumnal leaf colour and they are very good value in this the dying of the year. A few clematis will still be flowering in sheltered sites.

AT THEIR BEST

Clematis flammula, C. vitalba
Jasminum officinale (until first frost)
Parthenocissus (Virginia creeper)
Vitis (vines)

CONTAINERS

- Plant spring bulbs and winter foliage such as ivies, pyracantha and heathers.

GOOD ENOUGH TO EAT

The vegetable garden should still be producing lettuce, and some beans and tomatoes will still be ripening under glass. Apples and pears are at their best, as well as autumn raspberries.

- Plant garlic, placing cloves 15cm (6in) apart, 2.5cm (1in) below the soil, pointed end up.

The intensity of autumn leaf colour is dependent on hot days and cold nights in August.

November

ONCE THE CLOCKS GO BACK, WORK IN THE GARDEN WINDS DOWN DRAMATICALLY. For many town gardeners there is little to do and days will go by without you setting foot outside. But there are often beautiful frosty days before all the leaves drop in which it is a real pleasure to be out of doors, and there are plenty of jobs it is good to get on with before winter properly takes hold.

GENERAL UPKEEP

This is the month for planting out deciduous trees, hedges and shrubs if you can and for marking out and digging any new borders. The more you can get done before Christmas, the easier it will be next spring. But keep off the ground if it is either frosty or too wet.

- Sweep up all deciduous leaves and collect them in black polythene bags. If they are moist they will rot down by next spring to make excellent mulch for woodland plants.
- Scrub paths and patios with diluted bleach to stop them becoming slippery with algae.
- If the weather is very mild and forecast to remain so you might give the lawn a very light trim, but it is better to clean the mower, oiling the blades lightly, and put it away until spring.

BULBS

- Plant tulips. These should be put in as deeply as possible – up to 25cm (10in) underground.

IN FULL FLOWER

Colchicum
Cyclamen neapolitanum

PERENNIALS

- Either cut back dead growth in the border, tidying it up or – as I do – leave it to encourage birds and insects into the garden over winter as well as providing a protective layer against really bad weather. Too much tidiness is a bad thing in a garden.
- This is a good time to plant ornamental grasses. Herbaceous perennials can also be planted now or left in pots until spring – as long as you can keep an eye on them.

SHRUBS

- Plant deciduous shrubs such as roses, as well as any hedging shrubs.

IN FULL FLOWER

Elaeagnus pungens
Erica carnea
Skimmia
Viburnum farreri

TREES

- Plant any deciduous trees such as fruit trees or hedging. Evergreens are best left until next spring.

AT THEIR BEST
Prunus x *subhirtella* 'Autumnalis'

CLIMBERS
- Plant clematis and climbing roses, as well as ivies and honeysuckle.
- Check all ties to see that nothing will be damaged in a storm. Check also the security of any trellis and wires against which climbers are growing.

AT THEIR BEST
Pyracantha
Parthenocissus quinquefolia

CONTAINERS
- Collect up empty terracotta pots and wash them, scrubbing with mild bleach solution. Store them out of the frost.
- Bring tender plants such as citrus and bay out of exposed positions in the garden, ideally into a greenhouse or conservatory.

GOOD ENOUGH TO EAT
- *Herbs* Dig up some mint and bring it indoors in a pot for use in cooking.
- *Vegetables* You can sow broad beans and more garlic (garlic needs a cold stage in its growth for the bulbs to mature and grow big).
- *Fruit* Plant fruit trees and bushes.

- *Salads* Use cloches to extend the season for lettuces and other salad crops, which should still be producing a daily picking.

A silver birch growing out of the silvery leaves of *Artemisia*. Both like well-drained soil.

December

THIS IS MY LEAST FAVOURITE MONTH IN THE GARDEN, the fag-end of the year when there are fewer flowers or signs of life than at any other time. The days are absurdly short, the light awful and the weather usually cold and dreary. Who would live in the northern hemisphere in December? However, this is when the structural planting of the garden reveals its worth – shapely evergreens, clipped topiary and shrubs with a strong outline give form and a green background to the garden in winter. Even without these, you can plan for next year, enjoy Christmas and let the garden sulk outside until you are ready to face it with renewed vigour in the new year.

GENERAL UPKEEP

Much of December's work is consolidating and trying to finish the tasks you began last month and could not finish through lack of time or bad weather.

- Keep sweeping leaves and storing them – they are the best possible conditioner for the soil. Burn all diseased leaves and woody material.
- If at all possible try and dig all new ground by Christmas. This gives the weather a chance to break it up before you prepare it for cultivation in spring.
- Make paths and patios as the weather allows.
- Please keep off the grass.

BULBS

- Finish planting tulips.

PERENNIALS

- Clear leaves from the crowns of plants but leave them in the spaces between plants.
- The Christmas Rose (*Helleborus niger*) might be flowering if you are lucky, but this is not really its season, despite its name.

SHRUBS

- Plant shrubs as last month.
- Knock any snow off evergreens lest they break under the weight. If you have an exposed garden, protect evergreens in extreme weather by wrapping them in hessian. But it is better to provide permanent shelter – cold winter wind is the number one enemy of all evergreens.

IN FULL FLOWER

Erica carnea
Erica darleyensis
Fatsia japonica
Lonicera fragrantissima (winter-flowering honeysuckle)
Prunus x *subhirtella* 'Autumnalis'
Viburnum bodnantense 'Dawn'
Viburnum farreri
Viburnum tinus

TREES

- Plant out any deciduous trees at the first dry, mild opportunity.

- Prune fruit trees. The idea is to cut free airways through any tree so that light and air can get to all parts of it. Prune espaliers and cordons so that the only vertical growths are short spurs.
- Do not treat open wounds with paint – they will heal better left alone.

AT THEIR BEST
All clipped topiary and hedges
Ilex (holly)

CLIMBERS
- Plant climbing roses and clematis.
- Protect tender climbers on walls by rigging up an 'eiderdown' of bubblewrap supported by chicken wire or polythene sheeting held in place with canes.

AT THEIR BEST
Cotoneaster horizontalis
Hedera (ivy)

CONTAINERS
Many plants will survive very cold weather provided their roots do not freeze, so protect containers themselves from frost by wrapping them in hessian or blankets and grouping them together to reduce wind chill.

GOOD ENOUGH TO EAT
There are still apples to collect for eating and storing. Salad crops such as rocket, lamb's lettuce and mizuna should give you a Christmas salad and evergreen herbs such as rosemary, sage and thyme can be picked.

Midwinter frost is no enemy to the garden, killing off pests and disease and looking wonderful rimed on leaves and bare stems.

Index